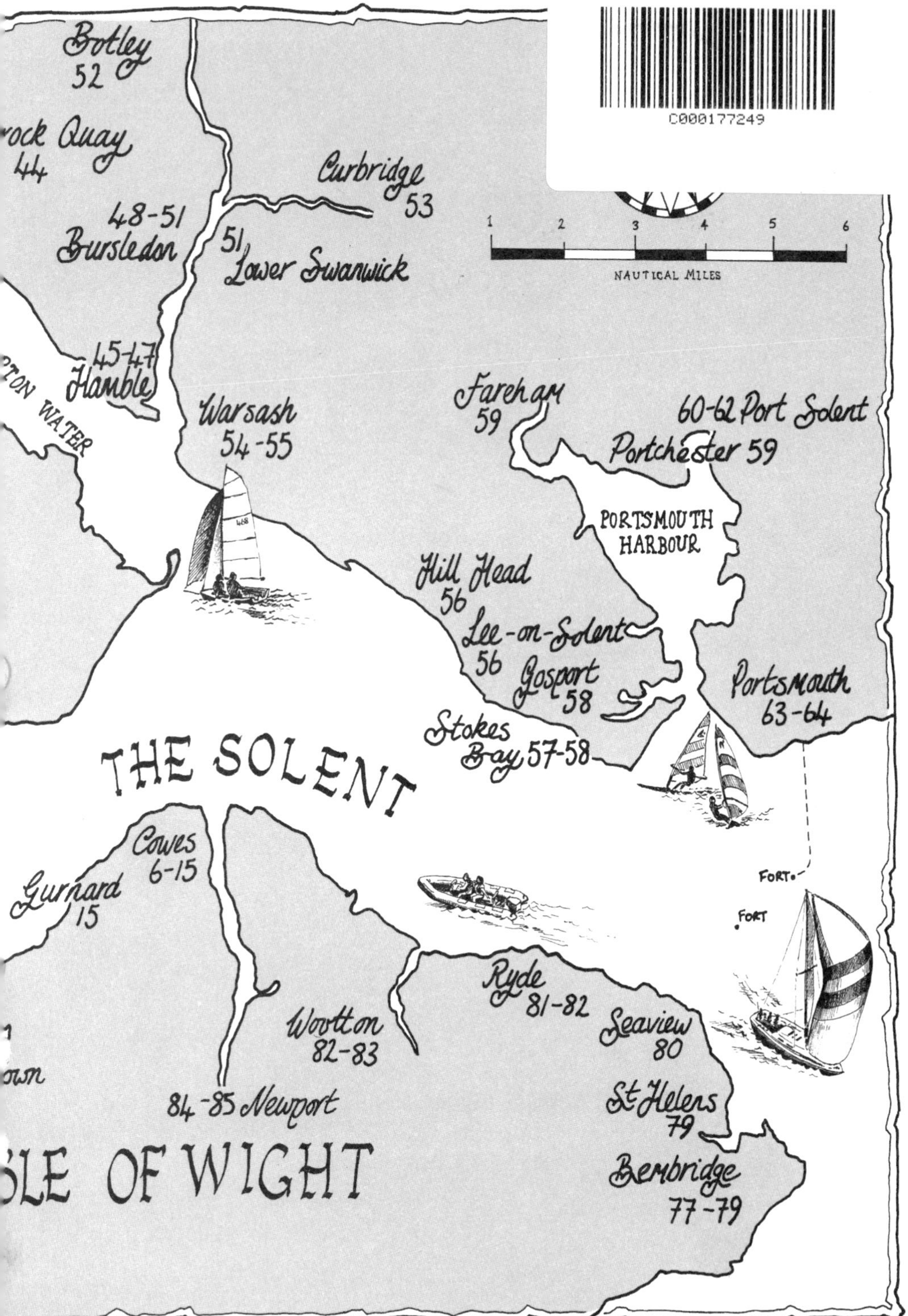

Botley
52

rock Quay
44

Curbridge
53

48-51
Bursledon

51
Lower Swanwick

NAUTICAL MILES

45-47
Hamble

TON WATER

Warsash
54-55

Fareham
59

60-62 Port Solent

Portchester 59

PORTSMOUTH
HARBOUR

Hill Head
56

Lee-on-Solent
56

Gosport
58

Portsmouth
63-64

Stokes
Bay 57-58

THE SOLENT

Cowes
6-15

Gurnard
15

FORT

FORT

Ryde
81-82

Wootton
82-83

Seaview
80

own

84-85 Newport

St Helens
79

SLE OF WIGHT

Bembridge
77-79

By Peter Bruce

First Edition Published June 1988
Second Edition Published May 1998

Boldre Marine
Kestrel Cottage, Shirley Holms, Lymington
Hampshire, SO41 8NH
Tel/Fax: (01590) 683106

CONTENTS

Acknowledgement

In obtaining information for this book one has freely sought advice from responsible mariners who live close by the pubs and restaurants described, and I am grateful to all of them. I also have received valuable help with the research from Peter Wills and Detlef Jens.

Printed by
Avalon Design + Print
Priory Park Industrial Estate
Christchurch, Dorset BH23 4HE

"BET YOU HARRY AND JANE WILL HAVE ALL PETER'S BOOKS BY NEXT WEEKEND ..."

INTRODUCTION

This book provides a source of good pubs and restaurants to visit by sea or land for food and drink within the Solent area. Some are chosen because they are popular and convenient for Solent mariners, and some because they provide a rewarding objective at the end of an attractive and interesting Solent voyage. Others look over bays where the bow can be put on the beach when the weather is favourable; or a kedge dropped and the dinghy used to get ashore, allowing one of the great joys of seafaring, namely watching one's own vessel lying tranquil at anchor whilst refreshment is enjoyed.

It should be mentioned that much of the information in this book comes from those who live locally and from managements themselves, and I am very grateful for it. One of the many questions proprietors have been asked is whether they do welcome visiting yachtsmen. To feature in this book, needless to say, they have had to give a clear affirmative. Such places are often popular for this and other reasons so it is always wise to book especially at weekends, to avoid disappointment or even mutiny. At one time it seemed helpful to show whether an eatery does vegetarian food, however they almost all seem to do so these days.

It has been generally assumed that, possibly encumbered with oilskins and seaboots, sailors will not want to walk far afield after a voyage; however there are some particularly charming taverns or restaurants worth extra effort, or even a taxi ride. In these cases the situation is invariably explained.

The objects of interest have been laid out geographically rather than alphabetically, starting with Cowes and the Medina river, going westwards as far as Totland bay, then back eastwards from Keyhaven to Chichester, across to the Island at Bembridge, and finally westwards back to Cowes. There is an index at the end.

Some navigational assistance is given to get to the places described, but this information is intended to supplement and not replace charts and other Solent publications. Moreover the book has been written with big yachts, little yachts, power craft, sailing dinghies and windsurfers in mind, so due allowance must be made for large draught and exposed sterngear. Needless to say as the approaches to the inns at the head of rivers usually dry out at high tide, it is only seafarers able to work tidetables who should take advantage of the more remote destinations referred to in this book. Robert Louis Stevenson said 'to travel hopefully is a better thing than to arrive', but in this case it may be best not to travel at all rather than fail to depart. Fortunately the Solent is blessed with a tidal stand which does allow some hours of respite after high water, but this means that once the tide starts to go it drops fast.

Inevitably pubs and restaurants change hands from time to time, have structural changes and alter in nature. The information given is believed to be true at the time of going to press, but new information and suggestions are always welcome. Amongst the many and varied places described in this book which number over a hundred and twenty, there must be one that is right for every crew, in every boat, in every weather. Bon voyage, bonne santé, and bon appetit.

Baan Thai

10 Bath Road, COWES, Isle of Wight (01983) 291917

Opening Hours:
6.30pm - 12.00 midnight
Takeaway: Yes
Children: Not under 5
Dogs: Guide dogs only
Payment: Cash, cheques, credit cards

The Baan Thai in Cowes has been popular for a number of years for the authentic and spicy Thai food prepared by Manee Spencer from Bangkok. This year, they have employed a new chef, also from Bangkok, who is a worthy successor to Manee's talents in the kitchen. Russell Spencer met her in Bangkok while travelling in his international advertising career. Somewhat untypically for Cowes, they have settled here more or less by chance, not having had any previous affinity with yachting. However, the small and intimate restaurant with its cosy ambiance is now regularly frequented by yachties, as well as the occasional boat-less visitor from the mainland. There is also a vine adorned, covered garden terrace which is a pleasant spot in summer. Naturally, they also serve the famous Singha Beer from Bangkok, which goes well with the food.

UK Sailing Academy

Arctic Road, COWES, Isle of Wight (01983) 294941

Opening Hours:
Premises always open during the season.
Bar open 6 - 11pm
Days Closed: November to March inclusive
Children: Yes
Dogs: Yes
Payment: Cash, cheque with card

The UK Sailing Academy's buildings were known to thousands of yachtsmen when it was the home of The National Sailing Centre. The UK Sailing Academy provides similar services to visitors as before and some of the staff may even be the same. The pontoon berths work on a first come first served basis, but except when class associations are visiting and such special occasions as Cowes Week and the Round the Island Race when one must make arrangements well beforehand, space will usually be found. There is only one metre at low water springs.

The UK Sailing Academy is open for showers and all meals, which are wholesome and reasonably priced, but the bar, sensibly enough for a sailing school, is open only in the evenings.

Murray's Seafood Restaurant

106 High Street, COWES (01983) 296233

Restaurant Opening Hours:
12 - until about 2.30pm
7 - until about 10pm

Takeaway: No
Children: Children welcome, but no special facilities
Dogs: No
Payment: Cash, cheque, Visa, Access, Diners and Amex

It is quite easy to walk past the Nat West bank without noticing Murrays beside it. Many famous Cowes people such as Max Aitken, for whom the inner door had to be widened to accomodate his wheel chair, Bobby Lowein and Jack Knights have in the past spent many a happy hour on the premises. It was started by Uffa Fox's nephew Murray Dixon and is continuing in the same most agreeable tradition. There is a very pleasant cosy atmosphere in Murrays and usually the food can only be described as delicious.

The Fastnet Restaurant

Cowes Yacht Haven, 124 High Street, COWES (01983) 299251

Restaurant Opening Hours:
All day in summer

Takeaway: Yes, full catering for yachts available
Children: Yes
Dogs: No
Payment: Cash, cheque, Access and Visa

If moored in the main West Cowes Marina, the Fastnet Café is the closest location where food and drinks can be found. It caters nearly exclusively for yachtsmen and is always busy in the summer months. It can seat 100 in the inside restaurant and a further 200 or so outside - which is especially pleasant on a summer weekend to watch the sailing world go by. The café is open for breakfast, lunches, and afternoon teas and the food has a reputation for good value. They also specialise in catering for yachts and events, a sample menu would include smoked trout and spit roast pig marinaded in garlic, wine and herbs. The regular lunchtime menu features light bites such as pizzas, lasagna, filled baguettes and jacket potatoes.

The Fountain

High Street, COWES, Isle of Wight, PO31 7AW (01983) 292397

Opening Hours:
Mon-Sat 11 - 11pm
Sunday 12 - 10.30pm
Takeaway: No
Children: Children's food is available
Dogs: Bar area only
Payment: Cash, cheque and all credit cards

Though once a coaching inn, The Fountain has long been popular with yachtsmen thanks to its proximity to the ferry terminal, the marina and, before that, the trots. It has been a traditional breakfasting spot for yachtsmen too weary to cope with a frying pan - though they now may have to book - besides being the regular home of Champagne Mumm during the Admiral's Cup series. In 1987 the winning New Zealand Admiral's Cup team used The Fountain for meals, as well as consuming, it is said, astonishing quantities of rum. There is a wide choice of restaurant and bar food styled as 'cosmopolitan'.

The Victoria Tavern

62 Clarence Road, EAST COWES
(01983) 295961

Opening Hours:
Weekdays 11 - 3 and 7 - 11pm
Sunday 12 - 3 and 7 - 10.30pm
Takeaway: Yes, prepared on request
Children: No facilities
Payment: Cash or cheque

The Victoria Tavern in Clarence Road is a delightful old-fashioned pub only about 200m away from East Cowes Marina, and especially popular with members of the East Cowes Sailing Club on Thursday evenings after their local racing. They are, no doubt, helped to feel at home by one of the bars which is in the form of a clinker built half boat.

The food is typically pub grub, with daily specials, substantial main courses, salads and snacks and has a reputation for being excellent value at reasonable prices. To help pass the time there is also a pool table and there are other pub games.

The Three Crowns

45 High Street, COWES PO31 7RR (01983) 280878

Opening Hours:

Mon-Sat	11 - 11pm
Sundays	12 - 10.30pm
Takeaway:	No
Children:	Yes in restaurant area
Dogs:	Only friendly
Payment:	Cash, cheque

Many Cowes houses have interesting construction and in the case of the Three Crowns, or The Plough and Furrow as it used to be, there are two old ships keels grafted together supporting the floor over the bars, one dated, allegedly, 1650. The recesses in the keel for the ships' frames are clearly to be seen. The change of name came about in the 17th Century when three foreign princes were unable to get back to their vessel anchored in the roads due to inclement weather, and spent a night or two at the pub.

The Three Crowns, centrally placed in the High Street opposite the Midland bank, has become something of an institution for yachtsmen and of late more of the younger species. Yellow wellies are welcome. In 1995 a new dining room was added by knocking through into the adjacent restaurant building making for more space for the frequent party/theme nights through the sailing season.

The food is good wholesome pub grub with the occasional 'blackboard' cooked by Caroline. There are some good real ales, the 6X being rated highly. In line with tradition bed and breakfast is available for those stranded by inclement weather or any other reason.

Bombay Restaurant

Shooters Hill, COWES (01983) 281118 or 280942

Opening Hours:
Lunchtime and evenings
Takeaway: Yes
Children: Yes
Dogs: No
Payment: Cash, cheques with card, Credit Cards

This cosy restaurant is tucked away in a corner on Shooters Hill just a few houses up from Corrie's Cabin yet still quite close to West Cowes Yacht Harbour. It is the oldest and possibly most popular Indian Restaurant in Cowes and certainly the place for a serious curry aficionado. The large and varied menu features several Tandoori dishes as well as some classics of Indian cuisine featured as 'Chef's Recommendations' plus serious curries and Bombay specialities. For those who cannot decide, there are also set menus for two or four that will allow the tasting of various dishes. The service is renowned for being easy and friendly.

Corrie's Cabin

Shooters Hill, COWES (01983) 293733

Opening Hours:
Mon-Sat: 11.30am to 11.30pm
Sunday: 5 to 10pm
Takeaway: Yes
Children: Yes
Dogs: Yes
Payment: Cash

From West Cowes Marina Corrie's Cabin is only a few cables' lengths distant. Go out of the marina entrance and turn to port up Shooters Hill, look to starboard and you are there. The convenient location is not the only reason for the popularity of Corrie's Cabin fish and chip shop amongst yachtsmen and Cowes residents alike. It is particularly clean and well run; it does all the usual takeaways and also has a small restaurant in a side room. The menu also offers other choices such as vegetarian nuggets, chicken nuggets, jacket potatoes with various fillings and much else besides. It is a friendly, cheerful and value-for-money eatery much beloved by the crews of yachts such as Owl.

Pier View

High Street, COWES, PO31 7RY (01983) 294929

Opening Hours:
11 - 11pm or later in summer

Takeaway: Possible. Sandwiches and burgers for example
Children: When space permits
Dogs: Dogs on leads
Payment: Cash, cheques

The Pier View is one of the great 'yachtie' pubs of Cowes particularly, but not only, appreciated by the Etchells Class. It has been recently refurbished, but nicely, and retains the local pub feel. It now has three levels, a lower bar area, the old snug bar a little above, known as the messdeck, and the top bar which doubles as an eating area and seat of the locals. Many will appreciate the new kitchen, the enclosed rather than outside loos and the central heating. Traditional standards are observed as regards open fires and absence of electronic entertainment. Whatever the secret of its success, the fact is that the Pier View can be very full at any time of the year.

Tiffins of Cowes

127 High Street, COWES (01983) 292310

Opening Hours:
Summer (June - Aug. inc.):
Mon-Sun 8am - 6pm
Winter (Sept - May inc.):
Mon-Sat 8am - 5pm
Sundays Closed

Takeaway: Yes !
Children: Yes - all sizes and ages
Dogs: If small enough to sit under table. Otherwise moor to lamp post outside.
Payment: Cash or cheques only

Tiffins calls itself a café-bar and as such does not fit the normal mould of pubs and restaurants though it does well as it describes itself. The beauty of Tiffins for the yachtsperson is that it provides an abundance of baguettes with 102 choices of filling, which make an excellent instant meal, for example when watching the fireworks from the water on the Friday of Cowes Week. Another neat move, if one has a mobile phone aboard, is to keep a menu in the chart table so one can choose from the vast list and order by phone from seaward. Filling, one might add, is the operative word, as few people can manage more than one Tiffins baguette at a sitting.

The Anchor Inn

1 High Street, COWES (01983) 292823

Opening Hours:

Mon-Sat	11 - 11pm (These hours may be reduced in winter time).
Sundays	12 - 10.30pm
Takeaway:	No
Children:	Yes, except in bar area
Dogs:	Yes
Payment:	Cash, cheque, Visa and Access

Most hostelries are busy during Cowes Week and the Anchor Inn, just about opposite the West Cowes Marina entrance, must be one of the busiest of all. Crowded it might be with yachties, but there is a pleasant atmosphere and the feeling of a clientele 'at ease with itself'.

The original house was built in the early eighteenth century from ships' timbers 'infilled with cow-dung covered lathes' and became the principal coaching inn of Cowes. In the early nineteenth century it seems that a master mariner made enough money in the slave trade to buy the premises at auction after which he fixed a large anchor to the outside wall: hence the present name.

It is a pub which goes on and on. From the welcoming front bar one can proceed to the middle bar where one can sit down for a good meal, thence to the back bar, once a stable, and which still retains the mangers and stone floor and now has pleasant and lively music; finally one can go through to the enclosed garden where one can eat and drink in the sun. Recommended, but during Cowes week watch where you put your feet, please.

Duke of York

Mill Hill Road, COWES, Isle of Wight, PO31 7BT (01983) 295171

Opening Hours:

Mon-Sat	11 - 11pm
Sundays	12 - 10.30pm
Breakfast	7 - 9.30am (by arrangement)
Takeaway:	No
Children:	Yes, except in public bar area
Dogs:	Yes
Payment:	Everything

If the Duke of York looks slightly austere, as it may do to those approaching from Birmingham Road, the impression is instantly dispelled once one is inside. It was built as a post house some 300 years ago and has been the domain of the powerboating present landlord for 29 years, which is believed to be the longest held publican-ship on the Island. Food is good value and there is room for several largish racing crews to dine with their supporters. Moreover the Duke of York offers bed and breakfast or just breakfast, the former of interest to RNLI trainees and the latter of possible consequence to those whose energy on the water by day is matched by their performance ashore by night. At breakfast one may be entertained by the cheerful wit of the locals whose affection for this hostelry is instantly evident.

The Traveller's Joy

Pallance Road, NORTHWOOD, PO31 8LS (01983) 298024

Opening Hours:

Friday & Saturday	11 - 11pm
Other weekdays	11 - 2.30pm, 5 - 11pm
Sundays:	12 - 3pm, 7 - 10.30pm
Takeaway:	No
Children:	Not near bar
Dogs:	Yes
Payment:	Cash, cheques, Visa & Access

Northwood requires a taxi for all but very enthusiastic walkers, placed as it is over a mile south of West Cowes. Although there are usually enough hostelries within easy reach of the river moorings to assuage most tastes, the Traveller's Joy, an old country inn, is something of a serious beer-drinker's heaven and well worth a little effort to get there. There is a choice of at least eight splendid beers, the landlord is tremendously welcoming and, by the way, did the 1997 Fastnet in *Amandla Kulu*, moreover the pub claims no less than two ghosts.

The Union Inn

Watch House Lane, COWES (01983) 293163

Opening Hours:
Summer 11- 11pm
Sundays 11 - 10.30pm
Takeaway: No
Children: Yes
Dogs: No
Payment: Cash or cheque

The Union Inn, a small pub to be found on the bend of the High Street just north of the Island Sailing Club, has become of interest to sailors on account of its good value and friendly welcome. Crew charged with going aloft in hazardous circumstances can take comfort from the fact that the Union Inn is one of the few pubs to be found with dedicated wheel chair access. The game pie is a bit of a special, and Gales Ales are available with the usual guest brands. There is a separate dining room to the rear.

The Folly Inn

Folly Lane, Whippingham, EAST COWES (01983) 297171

Restaurant Opening Hours:
Breakfast: 9 - 11am
Meals: Noon - 10pm
Takeaway: Yes, on request
Children: Yes, there is also a family room
Dogs: Yes
Payment: Cash, cheque, Access and Visa

The Folly Inn is an especially popular destination for yachtsmen, as it is pleasantly situated up-river of Cowes with its own pontoon. Further berths are available on the piles in mid-stream. The south end of the pontoon is deepest, with over a metre at low water neaps. More water will be found out on the piles. If going for a pile berth at low tide, the best water will be found on the west side of the channel and at piles numbering 1 to 10. A water taxi operates at specific times to allow those on the piles to land without using a dinghy. The Folly is open all day, serving full breakfasts from 9 to 11am, as well as hearty lunches and evening meals later on, with grills and a good variety of quality pub food. The half shoulder of lamb and the Folly hog of pork rate high among the favourites. There is also a children's' menu. Showers are available from 8 in the morning, there is a weather station and fresh water may also be obtained.

The Woodvale

1 Princes Esplanade, GURNARD PO1 8LE (01983) 292037

Opening Hours:
Mon-Sat 11 - 11pm
Sundays 12 - 10.30pm
Takeaway: No
Children: Yes
Dogs: Yes if on a lead
Payment: Cash and cheques with card

Besides being a useful landmark when at sea to avoid colliding with Gurnard Ledge, The Woodvale is in a prime position to watch a Cowes based race for yachts and power boats or just to watch the sunset. There are times when Gurnard Bay is like a mill pond and one can land on the beach in comfort, but as there are a large number of pipes and cables running over to the mainland from Gurnard Bay, it is neither wise nor permissible to anchor there; though it has to be admitted that, perhaps armed with intimate knowledge of the seabed, some seem to get away with it. Within The Woodvale will be found traditional ale, very tasty hot and cold snacks - so the locals say, and seafood.

The New Inn

Shalfleet, NEWTOWN, Isle of Wight (01983) 531314

Opening Hours:
Winter:
Mon-Sat 11am - 3pm, 6 - 11pm
Sundays 12 - 2pm, 7 - 10.30pm
Summer:
Open all day, seven days a week
Takeaway: No
Children: Yes
Dogs: Yes
Payment: Cash, cheque & most cards

The New Inn at Shalfleet is in fact very old, having been mentioned in the Domesday book, and retains a venerable and charming character. It used to be one of the great delights of the Solent. Indeed amongst the cognoscente of Lymington, high water at a convenient time to visit the New Inn was called a 'brewer's tide'. Nowadays the pub has become so popular that the standards of byegone years have faded.

A dinghy is necessary, or shoal drafted boat, and one should land at Shalfleet Quay and walk up the path by the creek. It is National Trust land and harbour dues may be required at the Shalfleet Quay boatyard, though there is no charge for dinghies. Over two metres of water will be found at the quay at high water springs, and dinghies can get in there for about an hour either side of low water.

The Bugle

The Square, YARMOUTH PO41 0NS (01983) 760272

Opening Hours:

Mon-Sat	10.30 - 11pm
Sundays	12 - 10.30pm
Takeaway:	No
Children:	Yes, in the family room
Dogs:	Yes
Payment:	Cash, cheque, Visa, Access and Switch

The 300 year old Bugle Hotel tends to be popular with yachtsmen and summer visitors. There are two bars: the Poachers lounge bar, which tends to be on the quiet side, and the much more lively public bar, which caters for the young and extrovert. Both bars work from the same menu. There is a courtyard where a barbecue operates in the summer. Given notice, arrangements can be made for large parties such as crew dinners.

The King's Head

Quay Street, YARMOUTH (01983) 760351

Opening Hours:

Summer:	
Mon-Sat	11 - 11pm
Sundays	12 - 10.30pm
Winter:	
Weekdays	11 - 3pm
Saturdays	all day
Sundays	12 - 3pm, 7 - 10.30pm
Takeaway:	No
Children:	Yes, in family room where smoking is not allowed
Dogs:	Yes
Payment:	Cash, cheque, Visa, Access and Switch

The King's Head is the oldest and one of the more popular of the liberal supply of pubs in the picturesque little town of Yarmouth. The building dates back to the 13th Century, and became the conveniently placed garrison quarters for Yarmouth castle when this was completed in 1547, and again more recently in the last war. The name comes from Charles I who, having escaped to the Island in 1647, involuntarily spent a year there before being taken to the scaffold.

The pub has been recently refurbished and more space found by making the old kitchen and scullery into a family room, but the character has been largely retained as have the log fires. Food is standard pub grub with home made pasta and traditional stone baked pizza the specialities. One has to look to the blackboard for home-made pie and fish 'straight off the boats'.

Saltys

Quay Street, YARMOUTH (01983) 761550

Opening Hours:

Summer	Lunch from 12am Dinner from 7pm
Winter	Long weekends

Takeaway: Plenty of scope downstairs, sea bass being a bit of a speciality
Children: Yes

Visitors to Yarmouth in recent years, heading up Quay Street from the harbour, will have noticed a wet fish shop on their left where the goods are presented in an unusually attractive way. The building was once the stable and garage for the George Hotel and was converted by islanders, Pete & Jo Green, whose supplies come fresh from their son Jamie's Yarmouth-based fishing boat, The John Edward, and other local boats.

Subsequently Jo Green decided to give up her social work and opened a restaurant upstairs, having first had the floor re-laid with locally collected driftwood. With a little help from daughter Nicky the restaurant has been a great success. After a week of gales, choice may sometimes be rather limited, but at least one can be sure that the fish is fresh. Jo says there is always one meat dish available. The bare wood structure and red brick walls seem to complement the general scheme of things, which amount to warm, pleasant surroundings and good value.

Wheatsheaf Inn

Bridge Road, YARMOUTH (01983) 760456

Takeaway: No
Children: Yes, also in the conservatory in the garden in summer
Dogs: In the garden if well behaved
Payment: Cash, cheque, Switch, Access and Visa

All the Yarmouth pubs are well run and good value, but can be quite full in the holiday season. The Wheatsheaf is no exception, being only a stone's throw from the harbour, but this large and typical Whitbread pub can cater for many people at any time. A wide variety of pub food is provided, the standard menu being extended by daily specials. There are plenty of tables and large groups are always welcome, though prior notice is appreciated.

The George

Quay Street, YARMOUTH (01983) 760331

Opening Hours:
Bar 11 - 3pm; 6 - 11pm
Takeaway: No
Children: Welcome in the garden
Dogs: In the garden
Payment: Cash, cheques, all cards except Diners

When entering Yarmouth Harbour, The George is to be seen standing prominently beside the old castle, built in the reign of Henry VIII, east of Yarmouth harbour entrance to keep out French marauders. To get to The George, which has moved firmly up market under its present proprietors, one may wish to take advantage of the efficient Sandhard ferry service, found on VHF Channel 15, to land from the harbour moorings. At one time it was acceptable to land on the beach in front of the hotel but prior notice is now asked for.

The garden now has waiter service. Food is good typical English with a seafood bias worthy, it seems, of AA rosettes and mention in the Good Food Guide, a fact which certain Lymington dwellers who are fond of going over to the George at the beginning and end of the season for a lobster lunch will be glad to note. In fact Yarmouth can be a most attractive winter visit, aided by the warmth of The George's log fire. Arrangements can be made for large parties.

The Red Lion

Church Place, FRESHWATER (01983) 754925

Takeaway: No
Children: Under 10's in garden only
Dogs: Yes
Payment: Cash, cheque, Switch, Access and Visa

The Red Lion is a traditional village inn with stone floors and a pleasant ambience in the old part of Freshwater, close beside the parish church with its Norman tower.

Coming by water from Yarmouth, it will be found that the Yar gets more and more beautiful upstream of the swinging bridge. In the upper reaches, wildlife prospers, and herons stand like sentries as if watching over this peaceful and unspoilt river. By staying in the narrow unmarked channel, which can be discovered with a little care, it is possible at high water to get right up to the stone bridge over the river at Freshwater, known as The Causeway. There is no easy place to tie up and ingenuity or beaching may be necessary. Alternatively, there is either a footpath on the west side of the Yar through Saltern wood and past Kings Manor farm, or a route along the east side of the river down the dismantled railway line through Backet's plantation. Both of these walks are attractive and fun, and indeed the more energetic can use the Red Lion as a resting place before going on to enjoy the magnificent views of Tennyson Down.

The Red Lion supplies a large variety of good quality, freshly cooked food, homemade specials and sandwiches. There is also a colourful garden at the back.

The Waterfront

The Promenade, TOTLAND BAY (01983) 756969

Opening Hours:
Summer:
10.30 - 11pm
Winter:
Weekdays 10.30 - 3pm, 6 - 11pm
Weekends as in summer

Takeaway: No
Children: Yes
Dogs: Yes, on balcony
Payment: Cash, cheque, and most cards

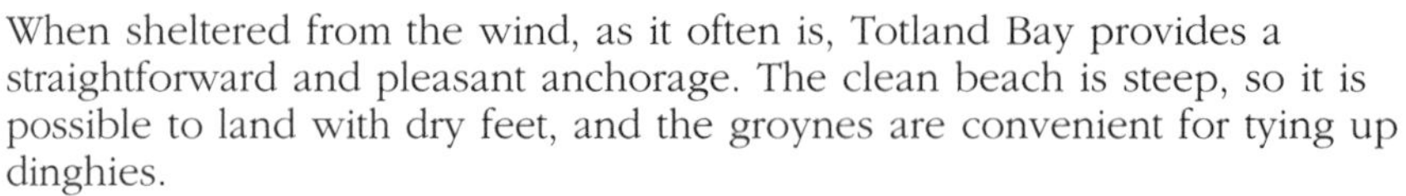

When sheltered from the wind, as it often is, Totland Bay provides a straightforward and pleasant anchorage. The clean beach is steep, so it is possible to land with dry feet, and the groynes are convenient for tying up dinghies.

The conspicuous Waterfront licensed restaurant can be seen just above shore level to the west of Totland pier. The building was built as the village church in 1869, but was dismantled in 1875 and re-erected on its present site. The Waterfront with its veranda makes a pleasant and convenient bar and restaurant for visiting yachtsmen. Of late it has become popular locally and has moved up market to become a little stretched at weekends. There are plans for a summer barbecue, and an ice cream kiosk. For a complete change of scene after a meal go up the lantern lit steps to the Turf Walk above.

Those determined to go ashore for refreshment at Alum Bay will find the Royal Needles Coaster bar not far from the top of the chair lift by a gift shop.

The Gun

KEYHAVEN (01590) 642391

Opening Hours:
11 - 3pm, 6 - 11pm

Takeaway: No

Children: There is an enclosed patio at the side of the pub and a large garden, both suitable for children in summer. Children's food can be provided.

Dogs: Dogs can be tied up in the patio or garden. They are allowed in the front bar if well behaved.

Payment: Cash, cheques or Visa

Keyhaven is popular with windsurfers who use Mount Lake, and there is a convenient anchorage for larger vessels to the east of Hurst. It can be quite difficult to find space in summer for a yacht within the attractive but tidally limited and unlit Keyhaven river. One can anchor just inside North Point or risk picking up a mooring but better to try to get a mooring from Tom Holt, the River Warden. It is possible to get up to the quay but commercial vessels have priority of use.

The popular Gun Inn, once a chapel, is some 160M from the quay, and owes its name to association with wildfowling, Keyhaven being the centre of activity for Colonel Peter Hawker, a celebrated 19th Century wildfowler who, incidentally, was the author's great great grandfather. These days the Gun has character and a selection of Keyhaven memorabilia. There is an enclosed patio which is used as a family room, a conservatory just off the snug and a large garden. Jacqueline Hill does the bar victuals, putting on seafood, such as dressed crab, in summer, and otherwise typical pub nourishment plus a variety of specials.

Rocher's

69/71 High Street, MILFORD ON SEA (01590) 642340

Opening Hours:
Wed-Saturday evenings 7pm
Sunday lunch from 12.15pm

Takeaway: No
Children: Over 7 years old, please
Dogs: No
Payment: Cash, cheque, Visa, Access, Diners and Amex

Having qualified at the catering college in Tours and doing Relais Chateau for some years, Alain Rocher came to England to learn English. The fact that he still here may have something to do with meeting Rebecca, now his wife, when he was working at the Chewton Glen. They have been providing a high quality restaurant in Milford for ten years and it is one of those places well worth a short expedition to find.

The building was completed in about 1885 as a cycle shop but has been a restaurant for over 40 years and is not without its charm but, of course, the major attraction is the French - based cooking which Alain describes as a touch of classical mixed with a touch of modern with emphasis on his sauces.

One can park in the High Street beside the restaurant, in the lay-by nearly opposite or in the main village car park two minutes away on foot.

Westover Hall

Park Lane, MILFORD ON SEA, SO41 OPT (01590) 643044

Days closed: None
Takeaway: No
Dogs: No problem
Children: Are welcome
Payment: Cash, cheque and all major credit cards.

Westover Hall is a grade II listed building constructed in 1897 for Alexander Siemens the founder of the internationally well known electrical engineering group bearing his name. After Alexander Siemens died it became the home of Lord Nuffield, alias William Morris, famous for the manufacture of motor cars.

Built with no expense spared to a design by Arnold Mitchell in the fashionable arts and crafts style of the day, it is an outstanding example of Victorian architecture. The oak panelling, the ornate decorative ceilings and the stained glass windows are a sight to be seen. It is now a hotel with 12 guest rooms with an unusually good restaurant.

Friends and relations of Colonel David Sylvester Bradley will be well acquainted with Westover Hall as this distinguished gentleman regularly invites his guests there for dinner. It is easy to see why. The hotel is run by a charming family who go to a lot of trouble to ensure that their clients are happy. The menu changes regularly, and maintains an enviable standard of excellence. This, the agreeable atmosphere and the beautiful view over to the Needles combine to make the ingredients of a delightful evening. It will take a taxi ride to get there, but the journey is well worth it.

Thatched Cottage

16 Brookley Road, BROCKENHURST SO42 7RR (01590) 623090

Open to public:

Tues-Sun lunch 12.30 - 2.30pm
Tues-Sun 'tea' 2.30 - 5.30pm
Tues-Sat 7.30 - 9.30
Closed January

Takeaway: Hotel guests can take a picnic to the forest in a wicker hamper
Children: Yes
Dogs: Yes
Payment: Cash, cheques, switch, JTB, Visa, Access, Master Card & Eurocard

Outside walking range of the Lymington River but somewhere to go for a special occasion is the Thatched Cottage at Brockenhurst. At first sight, the Thatched Cottage looks like a pretty, cosy teashop, as indeed it was for a hundred years. Since Margaret Matysik and her three sons have been there, some nine years at the time of writing, it has developed into a deluxe small hotel and restaurant which has won an enviable reputation, and features with approbation in quality national newspapers. Actually it still provides rather yummy champagne cream teas as well.

Food in the restaurant is favourably influenced by the families' long international association with Hilton hotels. In particular there is a welcome Japanese element on the menu as a result of Michiyo who married Martin Matysik after meeting at the Tokio Hilton.

The kitchen opens onto the dining room and those guests who want to become more involved with the cooking may, unusually, have culinary instruction before their meal. Everything that can be, is made on the premises.

Outside catering is possible and reservations may require a deposit.

Le Poussin

57 Brookley Road, BROCKENHURST (01590) 623063

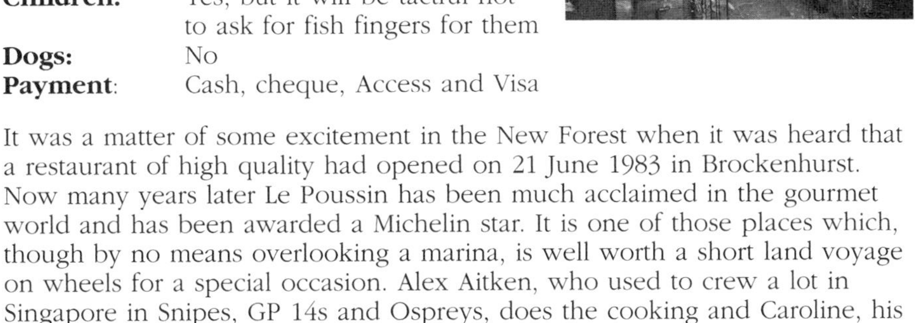

Opening Hours:
Tue-Sat Lunch 12 - 2pm
Dinner 7 - 10pm
Also Sundays and Mondays on Bank Holiday weekend.
Days Closed: Three weeks in January
Takeaway: Deliveries can also arranged
Children: Yes, but it will be tactful not to ask for fish fingers for them
Dogs: No
Payment: Cash, cheque, Access and Visa

It was a matter of some excitement in the New Forest when it was heard that a restaurant of high quality had opened on 21 June 1983 in Brockenhurst. Now many years later Le Poussin has been much acclaimed in the gourmet world and has been awarded a Michelin star. It is one of those places which, though by no means overlooking a marina, is well worth a short land voyage on wheels for a special occasion. Alex Aitken, who used to crew a lot in Singapore in Snipes, GP 14s and Ospreys, does the cooking and Caroline, his wife, who comes from the Isle of Wight, does the front of the house. It is always necessary to book, and visiting yachtsmen without transport will usually find that the Aitkens are able to get them home.

Provence Restaurant at Gordleton Mill

Silver Street, Sway, LYMINGTON (01590) 682219

Opening Hours:
Lunch 12.30 - 2pm
Dinner 7.30 - 10.00pm
Days Closed: All January, Sunday evenings and Mondays
Takeaway: No
Children: Not really, except grown up children for Sunday lunch
Dogs: No
Payment: cheques with card, Access, Visa and Diners

This Provence restaurant at Gordleton Mill on the Avon Water is an attractively renovated 17th Century building with over five acres of gardens, and amongst other things of interest to mariners, an ancient local chart on the wall of the bar. The Provence has a conservatory-styled restaurant with impeccable service. The cuisine is decidedly up-market though not as extraordinarily good as in the days of Jean-Pierre Novi. It is the sort of place for a special occasion, and worth the two mile trip out of town. A walk in the garden is recommended in fine weather.

Chequers Inn

Lower Woodside, LYMINGTON SO41 8AH (01590) 673415

Opening Hours:
Weekdays 11-3pm, 6-11pm
Weekends 11-11pm

Takeaway: No
Children: Yes
Dogs: Yes, but not in the restaurant area
Payment: Cash, cheque, Access and Visa

The Chequers was the exchequer for the salt pans on Pennington marshes, and dates back to 1650. Its existence once depended upon a deficiency in British weaponry, as on 18 December 1914 the inn was struck by a rogue shell fired from Fort Victoria which failed to explode, a shortcoming in British shells noted at the Battle of Jutland.

Though it is some way from the beaten track, and a longish walk from the Lymington marinas, the Chequers deserves mention as a principal meeting ground for yacht racing crews and their supporters. If ever there was a yachting pub - albeit a racing oriented one - this is it. Not only do many of Lymington's yachting names patronise The Chequers but others from distant lands.

If bent on adventure one can get to the Chequers by dinghy at high water. Follow the sea wall round from the Lymington Yacht Haven to Oxey Lake, then head south-west for the lock gate on the inlet which leads up to Ridgeway Lane. Leave the boat at the lock and take either path at the side of the inlet, the south one being the most direct. It is an attractive walk overlooking the marshes and can take little over five minutes. One can make the yet more ambitious trip from Keyhaven at high water too, but the options for pilotage are such that reference to a learned book called Solent Hazards v.4 is recommended. If all else fails, and one happens to have one's hand-held GPS, tap in the Way Point 50°44.'44N, 1°32'.63W.

Landlord and 'retired ocean racer', Mike Jamieson, runs a barbecue in summer, a small well-chosen list of wine and a good range of real ales. Bar food is home-made and the restaurant food is traditional English at the top end of pub fare, specialities being moules and fresh fish. Concessions are made with meal times for sailors taking part in the local winter racing series.

The Mayflower Hotel

King's Saltern Road, LYMINGTON S041 3QD (01590) 672160

Opening Hours:
8am - 11pm
Takeaway: No
Children: Yes. Family area indoors and outside
Dogs: Yes
Payment: Cash, cheque, Visa and Access

The Mayflower Hotel, a stone's throw from the Royal Lymington Yacht Club, the Lymington Town Sailing Club, the car park and the slipway, is said to be named after one of the early Lymington-Yarmouth ferries. In spite of its commanding situation river-wise, for many years The Mayflower Hotel did not cater for yachtsmen; in fact it was never very certain who it did cater for. Nowadays it clearly aims to be a family pub but has also steadily found increasing favour with the itinerant yachtsman, in particular supplying breakfast to those sailors at the Yacht Haven who are unwilling or unable to provide for themselves. Such has been the demand for this service that booking is said to be necessary. With a massive amount of space both inside and out, one would imagine that there is plenty of scope for winning more customers. Food is above average pub, a barbecue operates in summer and children's meals start at 99p.

Lal Quilla

135-136 High Street, LYMINGTON (01590) 671681 or 676924

Opening Hours:
12 - 2.30pm, 6 - 12pm all week
Takeaway: Yes
Children: Welcome
Dogs: No
Payment: Cash, cheque and usual cards

Lal Quilla means 'red foot' which has historic significance, but exactly what this might be has defeated those present from whom enquiries were made. Most of the world is more likely to be otherwise interested when they are feeling hungry, so we may never know. Anyhow this Indian restaurant has been in being for many years, and is conveniently placed for those yachtsmen operating from the town quay.

By any standards the quality of the food is good, and some find the takeaway facility particularly useful. An order can be phoned in and, at the appropriate time, a runner sent to collect so one can eat on board in the evening sun. There is a 10% discount for takeaway food.

The Hobler

Battramsley, LYMINGTON (01590) 623291

Days closed: Christmas night
Takeaway: Can do
Children: Not in the pub, but welcome in the garden where there are children's facilities and a variety of pub owned livestock in the neighbouring field to watch. In summer a marquee goes up in the garden and barbecues are held at weekends.
Dogs: Only the pub dog is allowed in the bar, others can be left in the garden.
Payment: Cash, cheque with card, Access and Amex

This pub is a favourite with many locals and visitors alike. Although located outside Lymington on the London Road some distance from the sea, it is much used by local sailors and as a crew gathering point before and after weekend racing. The name of this pub comes from a story that a lookout appointed to act as a communications link in the event of a French invasion used to hobble his horse and leave it to graze on Setley Plain. The building is about 450 years old and was once combined as a butcher and bakers shop as well as a pub.

Nowadays, the interior is particularly cosy and with its low beamed ceilings, stone floors and live fireplace it emanates all the charm associated with such an ancient building. The pub is usually packed with a lively and cheerful clientele especially on Tuesdays (Jazz band night) and Thursdays (Pop band night). On these evenings it would be wise to book a table early, say for around seven o'clock, if you want to be sure of getting a taste of the very good food. The menu is imaginative and changes every Thursday, and the quantity is such that few yachting gorillas are likely to go hungry. The Hobler was once nominated as wine pub of the year but also offers a choice of 100 blended and malt whiskies. It is well worth the 10-minute taxi ride from the boat for an eventful run ashore.

The Fisherman's Rest

All Saints Road, LYMINGTON (01590) 678931

Restaurant Opening Hours:
12 - 2 pm, 7 - 10 pm
All day Sunday

Takeaway: If required, also outside catering
Children: Yes
Dogs: Yes
Payment: Cash, cheque, Visa and Access

This old pub, formerly called Gratten's Cottage, has been popular for many years with yachtsmen, both as a pub and restaurant. Although located outside the town-centre of Lymington, it is not a far walk from the Yacht Haven. Back in the last war Vera Lynn, being a friend of the landlord of the day, used to visit and sing in the bar. There is a wide selection of real ales and good quality food, with fresh fish, seafood, meaty roasts all on the extensive à la carte menu and daily specials from £4.95. For the less hungry, there are also filled baguettes, sandwiches and bar snacks.

King's Head

Quay Hill, LYMINGTON, SO41 3AR (01590) 672709

Opening Hours:
Mon-Sat 11 - 3pm, 5.30 - 11pm
Sunday 12 - 3pm, 7 - 10.30pm

Takeaway: No
Children: Yes
Dogs: Yes
Payment: Cash, Visa, Access and Switch

This 18th Century pub will be found at the top of Lymington's picturesque Quay Hill; and it is popular amongst both locals and those using the visitors' berths at the Town Quay. After his famous circumnavigation in 1967-68, Sir Alec Rose worked on his book My Lively Lady for some weeks at Brackens in Captain's Row, then the home of the Nautical Publishing Company, and frequently had lunch at the King's Head which he found pleasant and snug. The King's Head has recently been extensively refurbished using old timber from the cellars, and during this work several discoveries were made. A well was found under the cellar floor, an oven dating back to when half the building was a bakery, and behind the oven a priest's hole. The pub has acquired a ghost, allegedly only visible to ladies.

The aim is to serve meals in restaurant style within a pub atmosphere. The food, which is all fresh and benefits from the proximity of the Lymington fishing fleet, verges towards the top end of pub grub and, together with the open fires, lack of machines and agreeable atmosphere probably accounts for the popularity of the King's Head. There is a patio to the rear.

Preacher's Bistro

Ashley Lane, LYMINGTON SO41 9RH (01590) 675370

Opening Hours:
Weekdays 2 - 2pm, 7 - 10pm
Weekends 12 - 2pm, 6.30 - 10.30pm
Takeaway: Can be arranged given notice
Children: Yes
Dogs: No
Payment: Cash, cheque, Visa, Access, Amex, Diners and Switch

For a restaurant which is rather tucked away Preacher's Bistro does very well and is popular with visitors to the Lymington river. This cannot only be because of the piano, which is bolted high up on the wall and is accessible to the pianist by tackle; a remarkably amusing bit of good fun. Further explanation probably lies in the pleasant lively atmosphere, reasonable prices and a style of food which appeals to the young and old.

To find Preacher's from the river, go well up the High Street until Lloyds Bank is sighted, then turn left into Ashley Lane from where the bistro will be seen on the right. The building dates back to 1664, and in 1791 became for a time a Baptist church from which association stems the present name. The food varies from Mexican to Thai through pizzas, pasta, and steaks, and one can have a two course special for £9.95. The 'hanging pianist', Mad Matt Black, is to be seen performing on Friday and Saturday evenings, plus Wednesday evenings during holiday time. Catering for whole crews can be arranged. Moreover Preachers also operates at the Berthon Marina in July and August at either the 'eating house' or the 'seafood shack'. These facilities are open to everyone, not just Berthon Marina berth-holders.

The Ship

The Quay, LYMINGTON (01590) 676903

Takeaway: No
Children: In the children's room
Dogs: Guide dogs only
Payment: Cash, cheques, all major credit cards

The Ship is only a warp's throw from the visitors' pontoon in Lymington Harbour. The pub consists of three cottages knocked into one and, although being of a somewhat average ambience, is a natural waypoint for the crews of the boats berthed nearby. Particularly on a sunny summer's day, it is quite pleasant to have a drink outside or in the adjacent beer garden whilst scanning the harbour scene, although it does get crowded at times. The Ship is not really a yachtie pub, it is the summer visitors who arrive by road, rather than yachtsmen, who dominate the facilities. The river end of the building is used as a restaurant serving typical pub food from an extensive menu. Showers are also available inside, and there is a dinghy pontoon giving direct access to those who prefer not to walk. Food is served from 11.30 through to 10pm daily.

Waggon & Horses

Undershore Road, LYMINGTON (01590) 672517

Restaurant Opening Hours:
12 - 2pm, 6 - 8.30pm
Takeaway: No
Children: Yes
Dogs: Yes
Payment: Cash or cheque with card

The mainstream of life in busy Lymington seems to be concentrated on the west bank of the river. However, the 'rive gauche' is also of interest especially to those seeking a change of scene nearby. The pub has benefited from a recent major renovation and face-lift and now has a cosy bar without being too far out of the ordinary. At high water, one can take a dinghy up above the railway bridge past Old Ferry House, which is a pleasant little trip in itself, and tie up to the railings beside the road. A stone's throw away will be found the Waggon & Horses so named because, before the causeway was built in 1731, waggons used to wait here for low tide before crossing at the ford. The pub offers good value for money, pub grub with a special two course lunch for only £4.95 on weekdays.

The Old Bank House

68 High Street, LYMINGTON SO41 9AL (01590) 671128

Opening Hours:

Weekdays	12 - 2pm, 7 - 10pm
Saturday	Evenings 7 - 10.30 only
Sunday	12 - 2pm only
Takeaway:	No
Children:	Yes
Dogs:	There are three regular dog visitors so one more shouldn't make much difference
Payment:	Cash, cheque, Visa, Access and Amex

The Old Bank House tends to cater for Lymington's professional people and lady shoppers at lunch time, and a wider compass in the evening. The restaurant is well up the High Street from the Lymington River, opposite the Post Office, but one can be sure of a warm welcome and a reward for the modest effort involved. The proprietors describe the food style as having an 'English base with international overtones'. This seems to be about right, and one could add that the level is above pub fare and good value. There is an attractive terrace for summer evenings.

Peeler's Bistro

Gosport Street, LYMINGTON SO41 9BE (01590) 676165

Opening Hours:

	12 - 2pm, 6.30 - 10.30pm
Takeaway:	No
Children:	Yes
Dogs:	No
Payment:	Cash, cheques, Visa, Access, Amex, and Switch

As can be guessed from the name, Peeler's used to be the Lymington police station and police helmets are displayed in commemoration. It is now popular as a restaurant, having a pleasant, warm atmosphere and cheerful service. One can have a whole meal, or bistro fashion, just choose one course. Cooking is fairly international: they have 'stolen a bit from everyone' they say. All the food is prepared on site, fresh fish, fresh pasta and charcoal grilled steaks being grist to the mill. Peeler's moules marinieres are notable and are much in demand. The restaurant will be found a short way down Gosport street on the left hand side when coming from the bottom of Lymington High Street.

The Stanwell House Hotel

14 High Street, LYMINGTON, Hants SO41 9AA (01590) 677123

Opening Hours:

Bistro	12 - 2pm, 7 - 10pm
Restaurant	Breakfast 7 - 10am Lunch 12 - 2pm Dinner 7.30 - 9.30pm
Takeaway:	No
Children:	Yes. Elgars cottage, an accommodation outhouse, is particularly suited for use by families, but there are double rooms too, high chairs, children's food, etc.
Dogs:	Yes
Payment:	Cash, cheque, Visa, Access, Amex and all other major credit cards

The Stanwell House Hotel is a three star Georgian Hotel at the lower end of the Lymington High Street. It has always been one of Lymington's better quality hotels and used to remind me of my grandmother's house of the 1950s: quiet, comfortable and spacious, in fact just the right surroundings for gentlefolk to engage in polite conversation.

As part of recent major renovations there is now a large conservatory, a wooden-floored candle-lit bistro and restaurant in addition to the old dining room. With the introduction of these new facilities the hotel has wider appeal. In the past the main appeal of Stanwell House to yachtsmen has been its proximity to the Berthon Marina. Another unusual attraction is the owner's 50ft yacht, *Alpha*, which may be chartered by patrons.

Harpers

The Yacht Haven, Kings Saltern Road, LYMINGTON SO41 3QD
(01590) 679971

Opening Hours:
08.30 Breakfasts 7 days a week in summer
Mon-Fri 10am - 11pm
Sat 8am - 11pm
Sun and Bank Holidays 8am - 6pm
Takeaway: Yes. Baguettes and sandwiches
Children: Yes
Dogs: Yes
Payment: Cash, cheque, Visa, Access etc. but not Switch

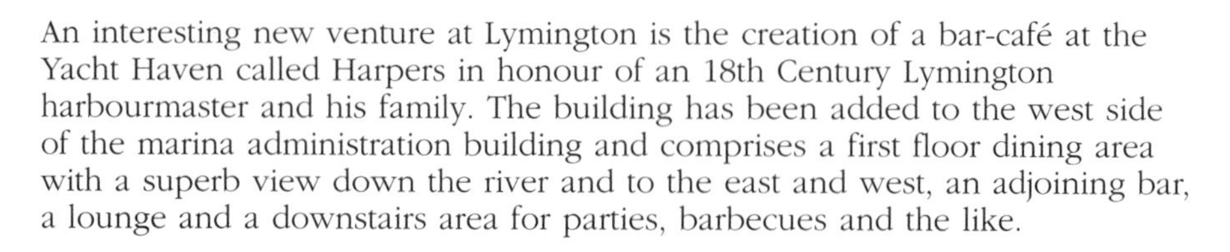

An interesting new venture at Lymington is the creation of a bar-café at the Yacht Haven called Harpers in honour of an 18th Century Lymington harbourmaster and his family. The building has been added to the west side of the marina administration building and comprises a first floor dining area with a superb view down the river and to the east and west, an adjoining bar, a lounge and a downstairs area for parties, barbecues and the like.

Harpers is run as a separate business to the marina by Frank Hardman who will be known to some as the co-owner of the Tripp 25 *The Light Fantastic* as well as the recent general manager of the Royal Thames Yacht Club.

One of Frank's nice ideas has been to establish a crew register on the Internet with a view to using Harpers as a meeting place. Racing yacht owners could find this of great help. There is a jazz band on Monday evenings.

Limpets Restaurant

9 Gosport street, LYMINGTON SO41 9BG (01590) 675595

Opening Hours:
12 - 2pm; 6.30 - 10.30pm
Takeaway: No
Children: If well behaved
Dogs: No
Payment: Cash, cheques, Access and Visa

A small, pleasant, unpretentious and popular restaurant of consistent quality at the top of Quay Hill and within easy reach of the Town quay. Robert Gray, who met Lynn when they were both at Bournemouth Catering College, does the cooking in French/Continental style, now assisted by Edwin Wateley. Their specialities are game and fresh fish, this being hardly surprising as Robert was once a local commercial oyster fisherman. He still owns a fishing boat called *Aurelia* which he keeps at the town quay and, no doubt, uses his fishermen friends to good effect in procuring his marine ingredients. Limpets is one of those nice places where if you ask for a really rare steak, this is what you get.

Master Builder's

House Hotel, Buckler's Hard, BEAULIEU (01590) 616253

Opening Hours:
Restaurant 12.30 - 1.45pm and 7.30 - 9.45pm
Takeaway: No
Children: Not in immediate vicinity of bar, please
Dogs: Not in restaurant
Payment: Cash, cheque, all cards

The Beaulieu River is one of the jewels of the Solent and sailing between its sheltered and woody banks is a delight at almost any time of year.

A natural stopping point for sustenance is Buckler's Hard which first achieved eminence in the 18th century as the principal naval shipbuilding yard in the Solent. For example in the period 1744-94 Beaulieu built 42 ships, to Portsmouth's 32, Bursledon's 19 and Southampton's 10. This success can be partly attributed to the proximity of good oak, and part the skill of the master builder, Henry Adams, whose house now serves as a hotel. One can dine in comfort in the restaurant, or walk another few paces up the hill and use the stone flagged, oak beamed Yachtsman's Bar where a log fire will be found in cool weather. There are two boards at the end of the bar, one gives a record of all the ships built at Buckler's Hard, and the other is much used by the Yachtsman's darts team. In high summer clients from the bar spill merrily out onto the grass outside, alternatively there is a beer garden at the back. The buffet bar opens off the main bar and provides cold meats and salads, soups and a hot dish of the day at lunch-time, and a wider selection of hot food in the evening. The hotel restaurant offers traditional English cookery with specialities of pheasant and other game. One can have tea outside whilst enjoying the view over the river, and also there is a thatched cottage called the Dukes Bath Club beside the river path to the marina which opens as another bar in the summer, and can be booked for barbecues in the pleasant and secluded garden.

It could be mentioned that those with young children in tow might find useful the Mulberry Caféteria up the hill beyond the maritime museum.

Montagu Arms Hotel

BEAULIEU (01590) 612324

Takeaway: No
Children: Not in the restaurant in the evenings
Dogs: No
Payment: Cash and all major credit cards

The Montagu Arms Hotel in the centre of picturesque Beaulieu Village has been fashionable for many years as a very civilised and old-style country hotel with a restaurant that maintains high standards of modern English cuisine. The ambiance is pleasantly sedate and most would regard the traditional restaurant as a fitting place for a treat. There is a set menu for £20 or £24 (two or three course), but a full à la carte dinner for two with an appropriate wine would probably incur a bill in the region of £100. The lounge or the conservatory of the Hotel is also a very nice setting for a stylish and relaxing afternoon tea. One can take the dinghy upriver from the yacht moorings at Buckler's Hard at high tide, or alternatively follow the riverside footpath. It is two miles distant, but the walk can be a great pleasure as the river and surrounding scenery is beautiful. If going by water one can land at Timbrell's Quay which is a brick wall with steps on the right hand (north side) of the river just short of the road bridge. There should be enough water for a dinghy two hours before high water and three hours after. In wet weather, Beaulieu is only a short taxi ride from Buckler's Hard.

The Lord Nelson

5 High Street, HYTHE (01703) 842169

Opening Hours:
Mon-Sat 11 - 11pm
Sundays 12 - 10.30pm
Takeaway: No
Children: Children can use the garden
Dogs: Dogs are allowed in three of the four bars, water bowls provided
Payment: Cash or cheque with card

This building within easy reach of Hythe marina is 460 years old and was once a customs house. It is reputed to have been visited by Nelson on his way to Bucklers Hard, and is the last of the old style pubs left in the attractive village of Hythe. The beams are adorned with a multitude of Royal Naval ship's crests indicating popularity within at least one group. The Lord Nelson also acts as headquarters for a football team, and collects for the Lord Nelson Jubilee Sailing Trust and other charities. The pub sports four different bars, one of them recently installed in the old cellar. Home made food consists of hot and cold snacks available lunch-time Monday to Saturday.

Hobbits

6b High Street, HYTHE SO45 6AH
(01703) 848524

Restaurant Opening Hours:

Mon-Thu	11 - 2.30pm; 7 - 11pm
Fri and Sat	11am until midnight
Sundays	Noon until 11.30pm
Takeaway:	No
Children:	Yes
Dogs:	Only guide dogs
Payment:	Cash, cheques, Visa, Switch and Diners.

Hobbits Restaurant Bar, once upon a time a wine merchants shop, and then a wine bar is located in the charming traffic-free Hythe High Street. It has a pleasant interior and retains some of the ambience of the wine bar which attracts nearby office people who go to Hobbits for lunch. Visiting sailors, who mainly come from the marina, are also frequent visitors, particularly in the evening, and are made equally welcome. One can also land at the public slipway at the south wall of the marina, though one should bear in mind that this is very stony on either side. Food is reasonably priced and there is a constantly changing selection of well-kept real ales.

Don Ciro

18 - 19 Shamrock Way, HYTHE, Marina Village (01703) 207730

Opening Hours:

Tues-Sun	12 noon - 2pm
	6 - 10.30pm
Closed on Mondays	
Takeaway:	No
Children:	Yes
Dogs:	No
Payment:	Cash, cheques, credit cards

This is a busy, popular and cheerful Italian restaurant on the water's edge in Hythe Marina Village with outside seating overlooking the yachts at their moorings. The Italian chef specialises in authentic and good quality Italian food, with many daily specials, all of which are freshly prepared to order in the open kitchen. Watching the chef whirling about his domain can be an entertaining way to pass the time whilst waiting for one's meal in the evenings when the restaurant is busy. But even at the most hectic of times, the service remains smooth and relaxed, with the waiters occasionally joining in with an enthusiastic sing-along to the music. The selection of wines is well above average.

The Mariner

37 High Street, HYTHE (01703) 847188

Restaurant Opening Hours:

Sun-Thu	12 - 1.45pm, 7 - 9.30pm
Fri and Sat	12 - 1.45pm, 7 - 10pm
Days Closed:	None
Takeaway:	No
Children:	Yes
Dogs:	No
Payment:	Cash, cheque with card, Access, Visa, Amex and Diners

The Mariner is a modern pub, built around 12 years ago. Its outstanding feature is the position and view over Southampton Water, which is superb. The new licensees have moved from a steak bar to 'English style' cooking and find that, to their surprise, cauliflower cheese is their most popular bar food number. They also do 8oz jumbo sausages, kebabs and grilled trout amongst other things, and there is a restaurant. It is a good place to watch for a ship to come in and, if one likes jazz, a good place to be on Thursday evenings when some of the best bands in the south of England perform.

The Boathouse Brasserie

29 Shamrock Quay, Hythe Marina Village,
HYTHE SO45 6DY (01703) 845594 fax:846071

Opening Hours:

Tues-Sat	12 - 2.30pm, 7 - 10pm
Sundays	12 - 2.30pm
Children:	Yes
Dogs:	Yes, generally preferred to children
Payment:	All major cards except AmEx and Diners

If you ask the social Beaulieu residents where they like to eat out, they may surprise you by declaring that this is at The Boathouse at Hythe Marina. On arrival the reason soon becomes apparent. Alchemist, artist and one of Britain's most colourful and better known chefs, Ian McAndrew, originally from Seaham in Sunderland, has set up business with his wife at The Boathouse. Food is in the form of small elegant flaversome portions which will delight those who prefer quality rather than quantity, a standard which is maintained even on the odd days when Ian is off shooting with his four cocker spaniels.

The restaurant, which was a pub before Ian and Jane arrived, is on two ground floor levels and has a pleasant atmosphere even though some may think it has been rather crudely nauticalised. There is a good choice of original bar tapas. A separate room is available for private parties.

The Jolly Sailor

Ashlett Creek, FAWLEY, Southampton (01703) 891305

Opening Hours:

Friday	11am - 3pm; 6 - 11pm
Saturday	All day
Sunday	12 - 3pm, 7 - 10.30pm
Takeaway:	Occasionally
Children:	In restaurant
Dogs:	Not in restaurant
Payment:	Cash, cheques, major credit cards

The small but charming Ashlett Creek is something of an oasis in the vicinity of the dominating oil refinery tanks along Southampton Water and well worth a visit by boat if the tide is right. The channel is well marked and over 2m of water will be found alongside the drying quay on a good tide. There is a maximum stay of 12 hours, and although some rafting up may be necessary, there is room enough for all. The Jolly Sailor is situated right beside the tiny harbour next to the old water mill, which is now a social club. Ashlett Creek and the pub itself are also well frequented in the summer by visitors coming over land, sometimes to the point of being crowded on sunny weekends. The Jolly Sailor is a no-nonsense pub in the best sense, with outside chairs and tables to enjoy those warm summer evenings. The pub was once called the Admiral Rodney as this illustrious sailor, who was victor of many fierce sea battles, had to join his ship from Ashlett in order to escape his creditors who were awaiting him in Portsmouth. The food is reasonably priced and of typical pub grub quality, with a self-serve roast on Sundays.

Deep Water Quay

Ocean Village, SOUTHAMPTON (01703) 230001

Opening Hours:

10am - 12 midnight daily
Food served until late

Takeaway:	Could be arranged
Children:	Yes
Dogs:	No
Payment:	Cash, cheques, credit cards

This waterfront bar and restaurant is a friendly, informal place for a casual drink or a tasty meal, and is conveniently situated right on the waterfront of Ocean Village not far from the Royal Southampton Yacht Club. The nautically-themed restaurant features an extensive menu and serves food all day until late - even if the chef has already gone, something can always be knocked up for hungry guests! The Bradshaw family who are incidentally keen sailors themselves, have only recently taken over and are aiming to upgrade both the food and the service - so far with much success, as their many regular customers will happily confirm.

The Anchor Inn

Eling Lane, Totton, SOUTHAMPTON SO40 9GD (01703) 863154

Opening Hours:
Weekdays 11 - 11pm
Sundays 12 - 10.30pm
Takeaway: No
Children: Lots of space outside, and family area
Dogs: Yes
Payment: Cash, cheque, Visa, Access and Switch

The shallow inlet at Eling is one of the happy surprises of the Solent area. After heading north past the container port towards the extremity of Southampton Water, at near high water one can take the well marked western channel, bringing one to this harbour of unexpected peace and charm. There is not much space between the many small craft based there, but one should be able to get alongside the wall within a biscuit's toss of the Anchor Inn and find about 2m at high water springs. One can dine either outside or inside on pub food such as scampi, chicken salad, or pies, and enjoy the local scene. At the end of the harbour there is a sailing club and the only tide mill in Western Europe still capable of grinding flour and well worth a visit.

Frog and Frigate

33 Canute Road, SOUTHAMPTON (01703) 335959

Opening Times:
Mon-Wed 7 - 11pm
Thu-Sat 7pm - 01.00am
Sunday 7 - 10.30pm
Food: None
Children: No
Dogs: No
Payment: Cash only

The Frog and Frigate retains the character of a dockland pub from years gone by. The only thing that really has changed is the clientele, as the Frog and Frigate is now mainly popular with students and the crews of visiting yachts, particularly in the evenings as the weekend draws closer. On Thursday, Friday and Saturday evenings, the place often features live music, or at least very loud music, and becomes packed with a fun loving, young crowd until 1.00am in the morning. A great place for a late drink and a good party, but not really suited to a quiet conversation, as one needs to shout to have any chance of being heard. All beers are £1 a pint on Sun, Mon, Tues and Weds. An entry charge of £2 is levied after 11pm on Friday and Saturday nights, but is obviously not much of a deterrent to its devotees. The Frog and Frigate is to be found just opposite Ocean Village: walk out to the main road, turn right, look left and you are nearly there.

La Regata

Town Quay, SOUTHAMPTON (01703) 223456

Opening Hours:
11am to 11pm
Takeaway: No
Children: Yes
Dogs: Yes - if well behaved
Payment: Cash, cheques, credit cards

Now that the refurbishment of Southampton's Town Quay is finished, there is a lot to be said for using its marina, especially if one wants access to the heart of the city. Just across the road from the marina is a restaurant which is just that little bit different: La Regata, located in the old warehouse building called Seaway House. The atmosphere is decidedly Spanish, with a tapas bar as well as a restaurant. There is an extensive and increasingly popular selection of traditional tapas which can be taken as light lunch-time snacks or be combined to serve as full meals. The restaurant menu caters for all tastes, the specialty being the Pescado Frito, a selection of fresh fish of the day served on a platter with enough for two to share.

Complementing the Spanish and Continental dishes, there is always a specials board with fresh fish of the day. To wash it all down in style, there is a good variety of Rioja wines, as well as Cruzcampo and Estrella in bottles and San Miguel beer on draft. This family run business was established in 1995 when Antonio, a restaurateur of 25 years standing and founder of Los Marinos in Ocean Village (where he won the Tapas Bar of the Year award in 1992) saw the potential of the Town Quay and surrounding developments. La Regata is run by Antonio, who comes originally from Seville, and his English wife Mary, as well as Pepe, Tim and Elna in front of house, with Manuel and his team in the kitchen. Due to its location, La Regata is often frequented by yachtsmen, especially during the Southampton Boat Show from which it is only a stone's throw away.

Los Marinos

Ocean Village, SOUTHAMPTON (01703) 335045

Opening Hours:

Summer	8am to 12pm daily
Winter	10am - 12pm
Takeaway:	Can be arranged
Children:	Yes
Dogs:	Outside
Payment:	Cash, credit cards, cheques with valid card

Los Marinos, situated right on the waterfront overlooking the marina of Ocean Village, has been popular for many years. It was started as a Spanish restaurant and Tapas Bar by the proprietor who now runs La Regata, opposite Town Quay. Since Mike Hyde has taken over four years ago, however, Los Marinos has been slightly more anglicized, without losing the Iberian touch altogether. The well frequented Tapas Bar has been enlarged, while the restaurant now features English as well as Continental cuisine and there is a large seating area outside, directly on the quayside. Particularly with the breakfast, served daily from 8 to 12 noon (April to September), Los Marinos caters especially for the visiting yachtsmen - Mike Hyde is a keen yachtsmen himself, having sailed on various racing yachts. He once also delivered the German Admiral's Cupper 'Tina I Punkt' from Ireland back to her builder's yard in Germany, after she lost her rudder in the notorious 1979 Fastnet Race and was left behind at the Emerald Isle by her regular racing crew.

Trattoria Ristorante Pinocchio

36, Oxford Street, SOUTHAMPTON (01703) 224444

Opening Hours:

Lunch-time - 3pm
Evenings

Takeaway:	No
Children:	Yes
Dogs:	No
Payment:	Cash, cheques, credit cards

Pinocchio in Oxford Street is an ever popular, excellent value, easy-going Italian Trattoria, serving good quality food without fuss: pizza, pasta, meat, fish, tutto va bene. This cheerful establishment, with its many colourful images along the walls of the restaurant that illustrate the story of Pinocchio, is also a definite favourite with many exhibitors during the Southampton Boat Show and has, indeed, also been featured in the Show Guide 'A Run Ashore with Seafile'. But Pinocchio can also get quite busy at other times, particularly in the evenings.

The Oxford Brasserie

33, Oxford Street, SOUTHAMPTON (01703) 635043

Open:
Lunch-time and evenings
Takeaway: No
Children: If well behaved
Dogs: No
Payment: Cash, credit cards

Oxford Street lies one street behind Queen's Park, which is about equidistant and within easy walking distance from both the marinas in Ocean Village and Town Quay, and is one of the areas in Southampton with notable gastronomic opportunities. In other words, Oxford Street offers a good range of fine pubs and restaurants, with some of the better known night-clubs and discos just around the corner. Outstanding even in this environment is the Oxford Brasserie, on the corner of John Street, for its first rate, Franco-Continental cuisine and easy atmosphere. Imaginative starters, some with a definite Mediterranean flavour and others decidedly more French, and mouth-watering main courses of well prepared lamb, duck, beef and fish are surely fit to please most gourmets. There is also a set £12.50 Table d'hôte menu. Larger crews should however note that a service charge of 10 percent is levied with all parties of six and over.

Old Orleans

Town Quay, SOUTHAMPTON (01703) 231733

Opening Hours:
Mon-Sat 12 noon to 11pm
Sunday 12 noon to 10.30pm
Restaurant open until 12 midnight
Takeaway: No
Children: Yes
Dogs: No
Payment: Cash, cheques, credit cards

The Old Orleans is situated right at the end of Town Quay, on the far side of the Isle of Wight fast passenger ferry terminal and especially convenient for all crews whose boats are moored in this marina. This southern style pub and restaurant is interestingly decorated and has a happy hour every day (Monday to Friday from 3 to 7pm), where some cocktails from the wide selection are sold for only £2. Extensive bar snacks and light meals from the Easy Day menu are served throughout the day in the downstairs bar area, including Nachos, Filled Potato Skins and Creole Pinchers (spicy crab cakes). Upstairs is a full restaurant with a substantial range of Texmex style food, with the sizzling Mexican Fajitas a definite favourite.

The Platform Tavern

Town Quay, SOUTHAMPTON (01703) 337232

Opening Hours:
Mon-Fri 12 - 3pm, 5.30 - 11pm
Sat & Sun 12 - 3pm, 6 - 11pm
Takeaway: Yes, on request
Children: No
Dogs: Yes
Payment: Cash, cheques, credit cards

This charming old village style pub with stone floors is situated right opposite Town Quay marina and one minute's walk from the yachts moored there. It has been a pub since 1830 but prior to that it has been variously, a poor house, a prison and a hospital. Recently re-opened, The Platform features real ales, a very good, world-wide selection of wines and superb quality, home-cooked food, served at lunchtime and in the evenings seven days a week. The pub is so named as it once was the site of a gun platform of the ancient city walls. The current building is still integrated into the old walls - a portion of which is glassed off in one corner of the saloon bar area. Old photographs and documents adorning the walls give further impressions of Victorian Southampton. The pub is much frequented by yachting folk from nearby Town Quay marina, and Alison caters for special occasions as well as crew gatherings and celebrations with her special mixed platters, even for the équipe of the largest yachts (although prior notice would help). She can also do takeaway hampers of her inspired Continental style cuisine. There is also some outside seating.

Yellow Welly Café

Shamrock Quay, William Street, Northam, SOUTHAMPTON No phone

Opening Hours: 6.30 - 6pm
Takeaway: Yes
Children: Yes
Dogs: Yes
Payment: Cash

The Yellow Welly Café, once a Camper and Nicholson yacht repair shed, can be easily identified on the corner of the main buildings at the east end of Shamrock Quay. Julia Jenkinson took over from her mother Rose Smith in 1990. Over the years The Yellow Welly Café has become something of a local institution by serving excellent and reasonably priced cooked breakfast-type food all through the day. For example the Britannia Sailing School invariably send their clients to the Yellow Welly for a good breakfast before embarking upon the week's instructional cruise. A focal point within is the pin board where customers advertise their sales and wants. Jobs are filled, crews for delivery trips are found, charter holidays are fixed and £30,000 yachts change hands through this free advertising.

The Bugle

HAMBLE (01703) 453104

Opening Hours:
Weekdays 11am - 11pm
Sundays 12 noon - 10.30pm
Takeaway: Not as a general rule
Children: There is a patio visible from the buffet area with swings, slide and climbing frame
Dogs: Well-behaved hounds with three 'A' levels are allowed in the front bar area on a lead
Payment: Cash, cheques, Visa, Access and Switch

According to the placard on the front of the Bugle, its history goes back to the 12th Century and the foundations are 800 years old. More recently the pub was owned by Winchester College which had rights to the ferry service between Hamble village and Warsash. Nowadays it is a plush place for tourists, businessmen and yachtsmen, the latter tending to use the front, or fisherman's bar. The buffet food perhaps owes its diversity and richness to the fact that the Bugle was one of the first pubs ever to provide food.

Ye Olde Whyte Harte

High Street, HAMBLE SO31 4JF (01703) 452108

Opening Hours:
Weekdays 11 - 3pm, 5 - 11pm
Sundays 12 - 3pm, 7 - 10.30pm
Takeaway: No
Children: Yes, in dining area
Dogs: No
Payment: Cash, cheques, Visa, Access and Switch

This listed building which dates from 1563 has beams taken from Tudor ships' timbers and an inglenook fireplace where logs burn in cool weather. Moreover 12th Century oak barn timber was found when the extension was done in the part of the building which for many years was the Hamble bakery.

Ye Olde Whyte Harte was refurbished in 1994 using all the old fixtures and is not really for old salts with wooden legs nor high-spirited racing crews: more the family-run pub for those who want to eat and drink in quiet and pleasant surroundings. To get to Ye Olde Whyte Harte, head for a minute inland, (i.e. west), from the square. There is a variety of snack food, restaurant food and a traditional wine list plus a choice of 21 Gales old English wines.

The Key at Hamble

Rope Walk, HAMBLE SO31 4HA (01703) 454314

(ex Beths) Proprietor: Mike Riley

Restaurant Opening Hours:
Lunch 12 - 2pm; Dinner 7 - 9.30pm
Closed Mondays & Saturday lunch

Takeaway: No
Children: Yes
Dogs: In the enclosed rear garden
Payment: Cash, cheque and all major cards

The Key at Hamble is an up-market restaurant in an attractive Queen Anne building, beside the Royal Southern Yacht Club and overlooking the Hamble Quay with especially good views from the upstairs windows. It used to be called Beths, but since then the interior has been altered (Proprietor Mike Riley's Turkish wife Duygo is an architect) to allow access to the garden from the front door, and there is now an upstairs restaurant called The River Room and two downstairs restaurants called The Gallery and The Pine Room. It is within a few minutes walk from Port Hamble Marina, and many yachtsman clients will have privilege of access to the Royal Southern Yacht Club's facilities for berthing close by.

The proprietor, who was for three years the chef for Sir Andrew Lloyd Webber or rather Lord Andrew Lloyd Webber as we should call him now, has had long experience of high class cuisine, and manages to produce superb food of imagination and flair. A summer barbecue, of equal standing, is available in the tiered garden. This has a pub licence and one can go there just for a drink though one is bound to be tempted to eat too. Like the food the wine is not cheap, but represents good value to those who appreciate quality.

The Victory

High Street, HAMBLE SO31 4HA (01703) 453105

Opening Hours:

Mon-Sat	11 - 11pm
Sundays	12 - 10.30pm
Takeaway:	No
Children:	Yes
Dogs:	Welcome
Payment:	Cash, cheque, Visa, Access, Switch

The Victory is 370 years old and a Grade II listed building. It has a flagstone floor in the public bar and a splendid mural in the back bar, depicting a scene from the Battle of Trafalgar, with 6 hidden faces to find if conversation lags. This, however, is rather unlikely, as The Victory pub is popular with the locals and visiting yachties. The landlord, who is reputed to drink expresso coffee from a pint glass, is planning a refurbishment imminently in sympathy with the present usage and character of this ancient building.

There is a good standard pub menu with a daily specials board offering interestingly different dishes such as nachos and piri piri prawns. Local fresh seafood is often available. There are six real ales to choose from and the choice of wines is ever increasing. One can book the back room bar for parties.

The Gaff Rigger

Mercury Yacht Harbour, HAMBLE (01703) 457220

Food Served:

Mon-Fri	11 - 2.30pm; 5pm - 9.30pm
Sat & Sun	All day
Takeaway:	Can be arranged
Children:	Yes
Dogs:	Conservatory and balcony only
Payment:	Cash or cheques, major credit cards

The Gaff Rigger is incorporated into the upstairs of the Mercury Yacht Harbour Marina buildings and is a pleasant, unpretentious bar and restaurant with prime views over the marina and river Hamble. A most attractive feature is the large balcony with adjacent conservatory. At the opposite end of the bar area, a new waitress service restaurant has only just opened up, serving sensible food at reasonable prices. Good lunchtime bar snacks are also available from a menu that features some refreshingly exotic dishes as well as the more usual pub food.

Riverside Chinese Restaurant

Bridge Road, BURSLEDON SO31 8AW (01703) 404100 or 405301

Opening Hours:
Tue-Sun 6 - 11.30pm
Thu-Sat 12 - 2pm
Takeaway: Yes
Children: Yes
Dogs: No
Payment: Cash, cheque, Amex, Diners, Access, and Visa

The Riverside Chinese Restaurant (ex Dragon Boat) is a good one by most accounts. It will produce both Cantonese and Pekinese style food as before and is not only convenient for those moored at the Moody Marina but there is also an adjacent hard where one can land by dinghy at half tide or more. There is an outside garden for customers in fine weather, from which there is a pleasant view over the river. Incidentally there is a fresh fish shop adjacent to the restaurant.

The Linden Tree

School Road, BURSLEDON (01703) 402356

Opening Hours:
Broadly speaking as usual, but shut in the afternoons
Takeaway: No
Children: Not inside
Dogs: Not inside
Payment: Cash, or cheque with card

It is really good to find a pub which has not changed because it has not needed to. Most of the indigenous yachtsmen of Bursledon have for years chosen to foregather at The Linden Tree (once known as The Fountain) for the best of reasons. Whilst not particularly convenient for those coming by water, the effort is justified. There is an appealing traditional atmosphere at The Linden Tree which may have something to do with a solid elm bar, attractive wood panelling, a real fire, besides Denise's home cooked and prepared food. Neither juke boxes nor fruit machines will be found. On the other hand there is a collection of ancient village photos which record, amongst other things, that Bursledon had a windmill and was in 1952 the all-England tug-of-war champion. Of more recent vintage is the inscription, lovingly carved by a local shipwright upon the beam over the entrance into the pergola, which classical scholars will find an unusual challenge. This is one of several imaginative developments undertaken by proprietor Roger Barrett whose gentle charm may also have something to do with the Linden Tree's long-standing popularity. There is a large rear garden, and a front patio under the pergola with a bright display of well tended blossoms.

The Fox and Hounds

Hungerford Bottom, BURSLEDON (01703) 402784

Opening Hours:
Weekdays 11am - 11pm
Sundays 12am - 10.30pm
Takeaway: No
Children: Not really a children's pub but there is a children's menu
Dogs: Not inside
Payment: Cash, cheque, all major credit cards

To the author's personal knowledge The Fox and Hounds and Lone Barn at one time was a favourite of young naval officers for wardroom outings, but its naval connections go back much further. Bursledon was an important shipbuilding centre in the Nelsonian age and iron smelters from this time were the first to use the 16th century part of the building as a pub. The site has been attractively developed ever since to include the Lone Barn, a medieval farm building imported stone by stone from Easton on the Downs above Winchester.

The current situation amounts to large and very pleasant premises well suited to crew outings with partners, and the like. There are no less than five log fires in winter and very welcome air-conditioning in summer. The trouble is that you will never find the place unless you know where it is, so you should be prepared to invoke the army saying 'Time spent in reconnaissance is seldom wasted'.

There is a much wider and more imaginative choice of food at the Fox and Hounds than one would normally expect, besides Dot Parson's chalk boards are a remarkable works of art. If you have never been to this pub, do so before you die!

The Vine Inn

83 The High Street, OLD BURSLEDON SO3 8JD (01703) 403836

Opening Hours:

Weekdays	11 - 3pm, 5.30 - 11pm
Sundays	12 - 3pm, 7 - 10.30pm
Takeaway:	No
Children:	Only on patio
Dogs:	Yes
Payment:	Cash or cheque

The Vine is the pub of Bursledon locals, many of whom have a connection with the Hamble River. Their choice in part may be because it is quite difficult to get to The Vine other than by walking. The low ceiling and log fire adds to the increasingly rare atmosphere of a good old fashioned village pub, the newish beer garden and patio being the only concession to modern times. Pub grub is limited to snacks except for Sundays when lunches may be booked. Beers are supplied by Marstons.

Badnam Creek makes an interesting and pleasant river route to Bursledon using a dinghy at high water. The creek will be found at the north end of the Mercury Yacht Harbour, and after negotiating the first bend one can see a pathway on the mound. This public footpath takes one under the railway line to the end of Salterns Lane which is a narrow quiet residential road adorned with daffodils in spring. Once up the hill one can either choose to turn right into the High Street, whereupon one will soon find The Vine, or turn left into Kew Lane which eventually will lead one to the Fox and Hounds in Hungerford Bottom, this having the advantage of the Lone Bar and plentiful outside seating.

The Jolly Sailor

Land's End Road, OLD BURSLEDON (01703) 405557

Opening Hours:
Mon-Sat 11 - 11pm
Sundays 12 - 10.30pm
Takeaway: Yes, given notice
Children: Yes
Dogs: Dogs are allowed in the front bar
Payment: Cash, cheques, and all major cards

After the television programme 'Howard's Way' the Jolly Sailor became known to nearly everyone in the country. Nowadays the pub is trying to live down its media exposure and is becoming once again an attractively quaint pub nestling in the trees. Having its own pontoon, where there is just over 2m at mean high water springs, it is particularly convenient to reach by water, especially by dinghy from Swanwick Marina. At the weekend when the tide is up, both the pontoon and the pub can be very busy at lunch-time, and it may be necessary to find alternative berthing either at the Elephant Boatyard just up river or the public slipway at the bottom of Land's End Road, which is just down river from the pub. A wide range of wholesome food is available from both the bar and the adjoining restaurant that operates in an old barn building recently brought over from Dorset. The river room carvery can be reserved for private functions.

The Doghouse

Moody Swanwick Marina, SWANWICK, Southampton SO31 7EF (01489) 571602

Opening Hours:
Mon-Sat 9 - 2.30pm, 6 - 11pm
Sundays 9 - 3pm
Takeaway: No
Children: Yes
Dogs: No
Payment: Cash, cheque, Visa, Access

This pub, as one might expect, caters particularly for those whose boats are at the huge and well sheltered Swanwick Marina. Apart from the undeniable convenience of proximity to showers, marina office and chandlery, the simple typical English pub food is done well and offers good value. Peggy Newman, who ran the nearby Ship Inn for 17 years, is well known locally.

The Bugle

The Square, BOTLEY SO30 2EA (01489) 781509

Opening Hours:

Mon-Sat	11 - 11pm
Sunday	12 - 10.30pm
Takeaway:	No
Children:	Small portions served
Dogs:	Yes
Payment:	Cash, cheque, Access, Visa and Switch

The attraction of an 18th Century coaching inn at Botley will not be apparent to most seafarers unless they should attempt a passage up the Hamble River. It is quite possible to get to Botley by small launch, or in a dinghy with a good outboard or even under oars, and is a grand adventure. One needs to set off for the upper reaches of the Hamble at least an hour before high water, to give some hours to enjoy the delights of the river, and eventually The Bugle. Take the left hand tributary when the Hamble forks and be prepared for overhanging branches and other challenges. The river is unspoilt and beautiful, as well as having a wealth of wildlife such as great families of wildfowl. One may also be rewarded for one's effort by the blue flash of a kingfisher in flight.

The river gets narrow, shallow and not quite so nice near Botley, where one may land at the old stone quay currently being refurbished by the parish council. This is about 150m short of the main road bridge at a tributary leading off to the west to a bridge under Church Lane. Alternatively, one can go right up to the bridge at Botley Mills. Follow the wall round to the left heading towards the mill culvert, and when almost upon the bridge, a secluded landing spot will be found with a large and convenient pipe to which one can secure.

The Bugle is a good pub, worthy of those who manage to reach it by water.

The Horse and Jockey

Botley Road, CURBRIDGE SO30 2HB (01489) 782654

Opening Hours:
Week 11- 2.30pm, 6 - 11pm
Sunday 12 - 3.30pm, 7 - 10.30pm
Afternoon times may be extended if the tide is up
Takeaway: No
Children: Yes
Dogs: Only in the garden
Payment: Cash, cheque, Visa, Access, Switch

On 5 August 1932 Curbridge hit the headlines when a Mrs Bone found a huge and active 'mystery fish' stranded in the narrow river not far from the Horse and Jockey. It was eleven feet long and may have been a pilot whale. Anyhow, what an eleven foot sea creature did in 1932 can be done by a shallow keeled boat now. On a sunny day it can be a very lovely trip up the wooded unspoilt Hamble River and then along its right hand tributary. Obviously one has to get the tide right, but that being so one can tie up by the bank opposite the Horse and Jockey, or use the pub's jetty and enjoy good food and ale. The food is good quality filled rolls and usual pub food with a roast on Sundays. The pub is owned by Gales Horndean Inns, an expanding chain giving freedom of style to landlords.

Curbridge Nature Reserve, open to the public, lies behind the garden leading along the river bank.

The Rising Sun

Shore Road, WARSASH SO31 9FT (01489) 576898

Opening Hours:

Mon-Sat	11 - 11pm
Sundays	12 - 10.30pm
Takeaway:	No
Children:	Yes
Dogs:	No
Payment:	Cash or cheque

In 1905 the Sun Hotel was built on the site of the Rising Sun to serve the naval base at HMS Tormentor, now the College of Nautical Studies, and the Victoria Yachts boatyard. In the 1930s the hotel was demolished to make way for the present building, known by some locally as 'the Riser'.

Some years ago this was a pub which could not readily be recommended to yachties, but now it is back in the nautical scene. David & Lynda Trivett are in charge, who some may remember from The Prince Consort at Netley. They have as regular customers those from the local boating scene and local young people at weekends.

If the Harbourmaster is called on Ch 68, or (01489)576387, and permission is granted to use the nearby Warsash visitors' pontoon, one is allowed two hours leeway before being charged, enough for most people to get what they want by way of sustenance. Dinghies can use the public slipway. There are large tables upstairs suitable for racing crews which will take up to 16 persons apiece, there is a shower room and a wet hanging space for foul weather gear, besides B & G wind speed and direction, Navtex and tidal data. There is even a skittle alley, well known to the author from his Navy days, which can make an entertaining focus for a run ashore given inclement weather.

Food is 'traditional English pub' with fresh seafood a speciality.

Jolly Farmer Inn

Fleet End Road, WARSASH (01489) 572500

Takeaway: No
Children: Yes. There is a play area in the large garden
Dogs: Dogs are allowed in the bar
Payment: Cash, cheques, Visa, Access

In spite of its distance from the Hamble River and un-nautical name this pub is popular with local yachtsmen. A visit entails a mile and a half trip out to Fleet End Road from the Hamble River via Warsash Road, or via Dibles Road if the Warsash Nautical Bookshop is on the agenda. The inn sign depicts a mortal with happy countenance and tankard, who shows a remarkable resemblance to the landlord himself. The likeness is no accident, and, indeed it is probably no accident that the Jolly Farmer continues to be successful and popular. The long-standing landlord, Martin O'Grady, is a gentle and charming Irishman who has created a place full of rustic atmosphere, where the food is more-ish and not over-priced and good real ales are to be found. One will not be alone in the Jolly Farmer, so it is well worth arriving in good time, though there is plenty of garden space.

Accommodation and breakfast is available for those sailors unwilling or unable to face the journey back to the boat.

The Osborne View

Hillhead Road, HILLHEAD P014 3JP (01329) 664623

Takeaway: No
Children: Yes
Dogs: Yes
Payment: Cash, cheque with card, Visa, Access and Amex

Apart from being a place where in calm weather one can land on the beach, the Osborne View serves two other useful purposes for sailors. It is a good lodgement for crews of shallow draught vessels visiting the tiny high water harbour at Tichfield Haven. Moreover, armed with a pair of binoculars, it makes a superb vantage point to watch the yacht racing which frequently takes place immediately off Hillhead, one of few places in the Solent clear of shipping routes and strong tides. Out of the sailing season the view alone is magnificent, and there cannot be many better places in Hampshire to watch the sunset.

There is an extensive menu and daily specials. Small portions are available as a light lunch or pensioner's portions. The Haven is not a particularly good place to dry out, so one should not dally long on a falling tide, and should perhaps speed return by using the bus rather than be tempted by the many seats along Cliff Road. On the other hand, if there is time to dally, there is a bird sanctuary to enjoy beside the lower reaches of the Meon River on the landward side of the road.

The Old Ship

LEE-ON-THE-SOLENT PO13 9BW (01705) 551038

Opening Hours:
Weekdays 11 - 11pm
Sunday 12 - 10.30pm
Takeaway: No
Vegetarian Food: Yes
Dogs: No
Payment: Cash, cheque, Visa, Access and Switch

The Old Ship building was converted in the '50s from a private house called 'The Gables'. It has Solent views and is convenient for the adjoining Lee on the Solent Sailing Club dinghy compound, the beach, and not too far away from the HMS Daedalus - as was - hovercraft slipway, now used mainly by water skiers. Those wearing wet suits, or indeed dry suits, are not usually welcome in pub bars but in the case of The Old Ship there is adequate outside seating. Food is good pub style grub, a speciality being a pint of prawns, with beer from Bass.

The Alverbank

House Hotel, Stokes Bay Road, GOSPORT (01705) 510005

Opening Hours:
Mon-Sat 11 - 11pm
Sundays 12 - 10.30pm
Takeaway: No, but an ice cream kiosk will be found to the rear of the building in summer
Children: Yes
Dogs: Yes
Payment: All cards except Diners

Stokes Bay is the home of all year round windsurfing and much additional water-borne activity in summer. Given the right conditions, Stokes Bay can make a satisfactory anchorage from which one can join in with the aquatic pleasures. Buried in the trees just behind the sea front will be found the attractive and elegant Victorian Alverbank Hotel, where one can dine in comfort in peaceful sylvan surroundings.

The house was built in 1842 for a Mr Croker who was the originator of the name 'Conservative' in its political sense. Among his guests were Prime Minister Sir Robert Peel and his ministers, one of whom was the Duke of Wellington. Sir James Graham, the Home Secretary of the day, lived in Cowes and used to land at a pier opposite the house to attend meetings. Lily Langtry, famous beauty and socialite of her day, was another visitor, hence The Langtry Restaurant.

Food is traditional à la carte and the imaginative bar menu, it is said, has the best Sussex Smokies for miles around. The New World wines and the constantly changing and well-kept selection of quality real ales are also commended. Whilst enjoying them, architects and others may care to note a rare example of a split flue chimney which runs around the west window of the bar.

The Pebble Beach (Bistro and Café)

Stokes Bay Road, GOSPORT P012 2BL (01705) 510789

Opening Hours:

Café	10 - 5.30pm
Restaurant:	
- Lunch	Every day 12 - 2pm
- Evenings	From 7pm Tue-Sat
Children:	Yes
Dogs:	No
Payment:	Cash, cheque, Visa, Access

The purpose built Pebble Beach Bistro and Café is sited at the centre of Stokes Bay waterborne activity, adjacent to Stokes Bay Sailing Club. Thus it caters for dinghy sailors, windsurfers, swimmers and those who simply come to watch. It is, of course, in appropriate weather conditions, possible to anchor off and come ashore by dinghy. There is a slipway at the Stokes Bay Angling Club 600m away towards Gillkicker Point and one next door at the sailing club. As a café one gets what one might expect - ice cream, cups of tea and buns, but as a bistro the Pebble Beach offers a wide and interesting choice of food with international dishes rotating about monthly and a serious traditional wine list. Moreover, should the proprietor's vivacious daughter be dropping by, one might overhear some epic tales of the Celtic Sea.
Given due warning the Pebble Beach can cope with parties, and offers a discount of 5% plus a complimentary bottle of wine per couple if the evening feature menu is chosen.

Ocean Bar & Restaurant

Camper & Nicholson Marina, Mumby Road, GOSPORT P012 1AH (01705) 503700

Opening Hours:

Summer:	
Mon - Fri	11 - 3pm, 6 - 11pm
Weekends	All day
Winter:	
Mon-Sat	11 - 3pm, 6 - 11pm
Sundays	12 - 3pm, 7 - 10.30pm
Takeaway:	No
Children:	Yes
Dogs:	Yes
Payment:	Cash, cheque, Visa or Access

The Ocean Bar & Restaurant is an integral part of the historic Camper & Nicholson yard and the bar was the old board room. Those who keep their craft at the marina find the facility extremely convenient, likewise those visiting Portsmouth Harbour, perhaps to view *HMS Victory* or *The Warrior*, both of which can be seen from the bar windows. There are bar snacks, à la carte meals in the evening and the wine list has recently been revamped. Fresh fish is available daily.

The Castle in the Air

49 Old Gosport Road, Lower Quay, FAREHAM
(01329) 280320

Opening Hours:

Mon-Sat	11 - 11pm
Sunday	12 - 10.30pm

Takeaway: No
Children: Yes
Dogs: Yes
Payment: Cash, cheque, Visa and Access

This 400 year old building was once the coal exchange served by the adjacent coal wharf. Not so long ago the traffic used to stream past the front of The Castle in the Air, but now the main road has been routed behind, and Old Gosport Road is now a peaceful and pleasant cul-de-sac. For access by sea, dinghies can use the public hard and larger vessels the marina 3 hours either side of high water. Visiting yachtsmen will find themselves much at home in The Castle in the Air, especially on the sofa in the 'snug' corner if fatigued by the middle watch, wind or wave. They will also find a good choice of fresh, home-cooked food and an all day breakfast special. There is now a patio for summer use.

The Cormorant

181 Castle Street, PORCHESTER (01705) 379374

Takeaway: No
Children: Restaurant only
Dogs: No facilities
Payment: Cash, cheques and usual cards, including Amex

Porchester Castle well deserves a visit and, given sufficient tidal height, there is no better way to do it than by sea. One can land on the hard on the east side of the castle, or perhaps if locally well connected, use the Porchester Sailing Club's pier. After exploring the castle, a happy bonus is that the nearby village is enchantingly pretty and well worth a visit. Though it is not particularly a yachties' pub The Cormorant will be easily spotted, and is well positioned for refuelling before starting back to the boat. A varied bar food menu is available with home cooked dishes of the day, but the bar can be a bit crowded in summer.

Charbar

25 The Boardwalk, PORT SOLENT (01705) 787978

Opening Hours:

Mon-Sat	12 noon - 12 midnight
Sunday	12 - 11.30pm
Takeaway:	No
Children:	Yes
Dogs:	No, except guide-dogs
Payment:	Cash, cheques and major credit cards - except Diners Club

This very family oriented BBQ restaurant can be flaming good fun for pyromaniacs, frustrated BBQ-chefs, bored kids or simply all the crew. Every table is fitted with a gas-fired, imitation charcoal grill where food can be cooked to taste, while the accessories (French fries, potatoes, salads and all side orders) are being served. Also quite unusual is the extensive and truly international wine list covering every area from New World to old Europe at moderate prices. There are also various beers on offer as well as crazy cocktails - even 'kid's kocktails'! Finally, there is the selection of 'flash it' snacks starting at £5.00, which are available from 12 to 18.30.

Chiquito

46 The Boardwalk, PORT SOLENT (01705) 201181

Opening Hours:

Mon-Thu	12 noon - 11pm
Fri & Sat	12 noon - 11.30pm
Sundays	12 noon - 10pm
Takeaway:	No
Children:	Yes
Dogs:	No, except guide-dogs
Payment:	Cash, cheques, major credit cards except Diners Club

This Texmex-temple sits in a prominent location at the beginning of the Boardwalk and features a nice terrace with commanding views over the moored yachts and the promenading folk on the dockside. Chiquito is part of an extended chain of identical establishments across the country. However, it is always good for a quick, fiery bite or an unpretentious, spicy meal. Inside, the restaurant has apparently been decorated with some nerve and verve, the result being interesting and colourful. The menu features Mexican inspired dishes, burgers and BBQ and chargrilled meats. There is a buffet lunch from 12 to 3pm Mondays to Fridays. Others might be more appreciative of the bar's Happy Hour, from 4.40 to 7.30 Mondays to Fridays, where a wide range of drinks, beers and cocktails is on offer.

Indian Cottage

44 The Boardwalk, PORT SOLENT
(01705) 214444

Opening Hours:
12 noon - 12 midnight
Food is served all day

Takeaway: Yes
Children: Yes
Dogs: No, except guide-dogs
Payment: Cash, cheques and major credit cards

This is a fine traditional Indian restaurant overlooking Port Solent from the upper deck of the Boardwalk. The cuisine is as one would expect from an Indian restaurant, but comes in well above average quality. There are two more 'Indian Cottages' belonging to the same owner (far inshore in rural Hampshire). A strong point is undoubtedly the large and well composed wine-list, which boasts 69 wines from most popular areas, many in the New World, as well as some exquisite Champagnes and vintages for the connoisseur. The ambiance is civilised, cosy and quiet, without being too flashy or over the top. Thus it is little wonder that the Indian Cottage at Port Solent becomes quite busy at times.

The Mermaid

15 The Boardwalk, PORT SOLENT (01705) 201012

Restaurant Opening Hours:
Mon-Fri 12 - 2pm, 7 - 10.30pm
Sat & Sun 12 - 10.30pm

Takeaway: No
Children: Yes
Dogs: If on a lead - but not in restaurant
Payment: Cash, cheques, Access, Visa, Amex

The Mermaid is a huge, purpose built pub overlooking the marina at Port Solent, towards the eastern end of the Boardwalk along the harbour-front. Its interior is quite impressive, with a central hall extending over all three floors that features a massive mast complete with gaff-rigged sail. Downstairs is the bar which also has self-serve pub food. There is a family bar on the tweendeck, with the restaurant occupying the top deck. The restaurant menu is quite extensive although not overly imaginative, with steaks, chicken, seafood and a salad bar, along with three vegetarian dishes and a traditional roast on Sundays. There is a wheel-chair lift to all levels.

Slackwater Jacques

16/17 The Boardwalk, PORT SOLENT
(01705) 780777

Opening Hours:
12 - late every day - but may be closed early if it is a very quiet night

Takeaway: No
Children: Yes
Dogs: No, except guide-dogs
Payment: Cash, cheques, major credit cards

Slackwater Jacques, located next to The Mermaid pub and somewhat in its shadow, is an easygoing, cheerful Cajun restaurant with an extensive menu of New Orleans and Louisiana specialities. The name, Slackwater Jacques, has no connection to Solent tides but is derived from a song by Carol King. There are Monday jazz evenings and an upstairs function room for private parties and conferences. In the summer, seating extends to the outside.

A good range of cocktails, from evergreen favourites to more exotic drinks like the 'Cajun Cooler', 'Hurricane Cooler' or the 'Long Island Iced Tea' (which has not a drop of tea in it) go down well with the spicy food. Open late every day, if it is busy enough until roundabout midnight with the last orders for food taken shortly before.

Pizzeria Ristorante Sorrento

19, The Boardwalk, PORT SOLENT (01705) 201473

Opening Hours:
Weekdays 12 - 11pm
Weekends 12 - 11.30pm

Takeaway: Pizza
Children: Yes
Dogs: No, except guide-dogs
Payment: Cash, cheques and major credit cards

This is a no-fuss, straightforward middle-of-the-road Pizzeria serving pizza, pasta and more all day every day. Especially handy for yachtsmen who may be feeling depressed by the English summer weather and who would like a little taste of the Mediterranean without having to sail all the way south.

Upstairs is another big restaurant with separate bar and seating for up to 80 people serving the usual Italian dishes as well as some specialities from Sorrento (near Naples). The à la carte restaurant is opened evenings only, from 18.30 to 22.00.

Still & West

Country House, Bath Square, PORTSMOUTH (01705) 821567

Opening Hours:
10.30am - 11pm
Takeaway: No
Children: There is a children's room, and children's food
Dogs: No
Payment: Cash, Visa or Access

The Boatswain's Call is a naval whistle which has been used at sea for giving orders since the Crusades. Its continuous high note, bringing the crew to attention, will be heard from Bath Square as passing warships exchange salutes with the submarine base at HMS Dolphin. This little ceremony is called 'piping the still' and accounts for one half of the name Still and West Country House. The other half came about through a marriage between the proprietor of 'The Still' in 1903 with a lady from another pub formerly known as 'The East and West Country House'.

The Still and West, once frequented by smugglers and the press gang, remains one of the attractive features of Portsmouth, and is another pleasant vantage point from which to watch the activities of the harbour. The food is rather more than typical pub fare, with 'specials of the day' advertised on a board, all served in a restaurant area. There is also a large choice of Gales olde english wines: apricot, cowslip, dandelion, parsnip, etc. in fact all 21 of them.

Keppel's Head Hotel

The Hard, PORTSMOUTH (01705) 833231

Opening Hours:
11am - 2pm, 6 - 11pm

Days Closed: None
Takeaway: Yes, a variety of carriage hampers with or without wine
Children: No facilities
Dogs: No facilities
Payment: Cash, cheques and all credit cards

Being just outside the naval dockyard gate, the Keppel's Head has strong nautical associations. Augustus Keppel (1725- 86) joined the Navy at the age of 10, and ended up as a Viscount and the First Lord of the Admiralty, having, amongst other things, captured the heavily defended Belle Isle and taken a distinguished part in the Battle of Quiberon Bay. Weather-bound yachtsmen at Camper & Nicholson can come over on the convenient Gosport ferry and use the Keppel's Head as a fuel stop before and/or after visiting Portsmouth's unique and wonderful concentration of maritime interest, such as the *Warrior, HMS Victory* and the *Mary Rose.* The Nut Bar is no longer and the hotel has been much modernised since the author knew it as a cadet and midshipman; but as this kind of young naval person is not around much anymore it may be just as well. There is a carvery and wide choice of food of Trust House Forte standard.

Spice Island Inn

1 Bath Square, OLD PORTSMOUTH PO1 2JL (01705) 870543

Opening Hours:
Mon-Sat 11 - 11pm
Sunday 12 - 10.30pm

Takeaway: Baguettes in the summer season
Children: Yes in family area and restaurant
Dogs: No
Payment: Cash, cheque, Visa, Access

The Spice Island Inn, once The Coal Exchange, is a building of great antiquity. It was called The Coal Exchange because barges used to tie here to exchange coal for local produce, using an iron ring still to be seen on the sea wall. Walls of an earlier building exist inside the present structure, and there is even a ghost. This is of the benign variety and allegedly is of a sailor who had an unfaithful girlfriend. The top bar and the public benches in warm weather are a good position to watch warships and ferries entering and leaving harbour. Moreover the helicopter landing pad close by is used by the Royal Flight from time to time. Such attractions mean that the Spice Island Inn can be very full at times, thus yachtsmen visiting the Camber should be timely in arrival to secure a good place to sit.

Topdeck Restaurant & Bar

Southsea Marina, PORTSMOUTH (01705) 874500

Food Served:
12.00 - 2pm; 7pm - 10pm
Takeaway: No
Children: Yes
Dogs: No
Payment: Cash, cheques

Traditionally styled unassuming and homely pub located above the marina offices, with a large balcony for sunny days. The restaurant serves average pub grub in pleasant surroundings which is just as well as there are few other watering holes within the near vicinity of Southsea Marina.

The Ship

Langstone Road, LANGSTONE (01705) 471719

Days Closed: None
Takeaway: On request
Children: Yes
Dogs: Yes
Payment: Cash, cheque, Access and Visa

If seeking a pub when berthed at Northney marina one can take a 20 minute walk over the bridge to The Ship. However at high water one can also berth right beside the pub alongside the old quay, built to take coal and corn barges, where one will find 2m on a good tide. The 17th Century building was once a mill, and the ancient wheel for getting the grain to the upper floor is displayed in the restaurant. Small craft can come under the bridge from Langstone harbour; and the old inshore route, the Hillsea channel, much used in the days of wars against the French, is still navigable for low profile vessels such as launches, and allows sheltered passage even from Portsmouth harbour. The speciality of the day is whatever has been obtained fresh from the Hayling Island fishermen; for example, bass, Dover sole or plaice.

The Royal Oak

The High Street, LANGSTONE (01705) 483125

Opening Hours:

Mon-Sat	All day
Sunday	1200 - 10.30pm
Days Closed:	None
Children:	Can use the garden
Dogs:	Yes
Payment:	Cash, cheques with card, Visa and Access

This attractive building started as a bakery in 1620. The front step is an original mill wheel and where ovens once existed logs are now stored for the open fires currently in use. In 1700 the bakery became an inn which it has been ever since. Food is aimed towards the top end of pub grub and a blackboard forms the only menu. The beer is commensurate with a Whitbread Wayside Inn with two regular real ales and two guest ales. The 'New World' wines are good value. There is a new patio to the rear of the building with views down Langstone Harbour and also a pleasant garden with rabbits.

Parking can be a little difficult adjacent to the pub, on the other hand if space can only be found in Towers Garden Road or The Saltings, the walk though the quiet village High Street can be a rewarding experience.

The Royal Oak is within walking distance of Northney Marina for those with a healthy appetite, moreover there is high water access to the beach just east of the pub for shallow draught boats which is well sheltered from the prevailing wind. The inlet dries out at low water allowing the occasional game of boules in front of the pub. Sweare Deep, the pool between Emsworth and Hayling Island, is windsurfer country for which the Royal Oak makes a natural rendezvous. Owners of dinghies from Emsworth Sailing Club and those with deeper draught vessels can berth beside the town quay opposite The Ship and walk down the path beside the sea. From The Royal Oak this path leads behind the grey towered mill to a bird sanctuary, which is open to everyone and a place where about 70 species spend the winter.

The Mariner's Tavern

Sparkes Yacht Harbour, Wittering Road, HAYLING ISLAND, Hants PO11 9SR (01705) 469459

Opening Hours:
Summer 9 - 11pm
Winter Variable
Takeaway: Yes - for sandwiches
Children: Yes
Dogs: Yes
Payment: Cash, cheques

The convenience of having an on-site marina bar and bistro is sometimes offset by lack of local colour. Whilst some might feel that the modern-built Mariner's Tavern with small patio comes into this category, they might nevertheless be pleased to find a pleasant club atmosphere where rallies for berth holders are organised and visiting burgees are always made welcome. The food is good value.

Spencers Restaurant

36 North Street, EMSWORTH, PO10 7DG (01243) 372744

Opening Hours:
12 - 2pm, 6 - 10.30pm
Brasserie Mon-Sat
Restaurant Lunch & Dinner Tue-Sat
Takeaway: No
Children: Yes in Brasserie
Payment: Cash, cheque and all cards

36 North Street was once the offices of Captain John Illingworth RN, the famous offshore racing skipper and yacht designer. Amongst many racing successes, he pioneered and won the first Sydney-Hobart Race in 1945, and his yacht Myth of Malham, which won the Fastnet in 1955 and again in 1957, was a new concept in terms of hull shape, displacement and rig. As Commodore of the Royal Ocean Racing Club he did much to set up international yacht racing as we know it now, and he was one of the prime instigators of the Admiral's Cup. When John Illingworth retired his offices became a restaurant which eventually moved to the Quay as '36 on the Quay'. However the Spencers took over at 36 North Street and so there is still a quality restaurant on the original site. This can be reached after a five minute walk from the quay via the High Street and thence across Havant Road. On arrival one has the choice of upstairs or downstairs, both gas lit, unless one has children in tow when downstairs will be preferred. Upstairs has won AA rosettes, and features in the Good Food Guide which describes the cooking style as 'modern French'. Downstairs, the Brasserie, is for the more casually minded but, at either level the food is of a high standard, and is strongly recommended by local sailing people.

The Coal Exchange

21 South Street, EMSWORTH, PO10 7EG (01243) 375866

Opening Hours:
Weekdays 10.30 - 3pm, 5.30 - 11pm
Saturdays 10.30 - 11pm
Sundays 12 - 10.30pm
Takeaway: No
Children: Yes
Dogs: Yes
Payment: Cash, cheques but no cards

The Coal Exchange - which of course, is what is was - is located in the centre of the village a short walk from Emsworth yacht harbour and an even shorter one from the quay. The attraction of this pub is simply that it is a good traditional pub with good traditional Gales beer and food. The menu is typical with a daily home made specials board. Food is available only at lunch time.

The Sussex Brewery

36 Main Road, EMSWORTH (01243) 371533

Opening Hours:
11am - 11pm
Meals served 12 - 2pm; 7 - 9.30pm
Days Closed: Christmas night
Children: Yes
Dogs: Yes
Payment: Cash, cheque, all cards except Diners

There is an abundance of pubs in Emsworth to choose from, but one worth seeking out is The Sussex Brewery a few minutes walk from Emsworth marina. Either go up Slipper Road and turn right at the A27 or, if the weather is dry, use a footpath over the fields. The Sussex Brewery is a locally popular small old pub which until recently manufactured its real ale on site. It is a Grade II listed building which, except for a gap at the beginning of this century, was a brewery since 1759. The floor is saw-dusted and the interior will be sheer delight to the traditionalist. There is a small, attractive enclosed rear garden which makes a good sun trap, and more seating in the two new dining rooms: one is for non-smokers and the other one housed the original brewery. Sausages are the food speciality of the house of which there is a splendid variety on offer. For example Drunken Duck which is made from breast of duck soaked in cognac and port, another from a recipe found in the Samuel Pepys library at Cambridge which includes pork and spinach and - assuming pheasant is in season - yet another 33 more, not including vegetarian, of which there are no less than six varieties to choose from. The sausages are free of the usual additives and are gently oven-baked to retain the full flavour. Parties of up to 30 can be catered for.

Thirty Six on the Quay

47 South Street, EMSWORTH (01243) 375592 or 372257

Opening Hours:

Lunch	Tue-Fri 12 to 2pm
Dinner	Mon-Sat 7 to 10pm
Days closed:	2 weeks mid-Jan, 1st week Oct Open Christmas Day and New Year's Eve
Takeaway:	No
Children:	Yes
Dogs:	No
Payment:	Cash, cheques, major credit cards

This is probably one of the better restaurants featured in this book and is about as close to the water as one can get, overlooking the busy Emsworth quay and Emsworth Harbour beyond. This dries out more or less completely, but there is a dinghy pontoon which can be accessed at all times except maybe low water springs, only a few minutes walk away. Tarquin Yacht Harbour, about five minutes walk or a short dinghy ride, has a sill allowing the yachts inside to stay afloat. Northney Marina, open at all states of the tide, is too far away to walk, but only a short taxi ride will take you to this gourmet centre. Speaking of which, Emsworth has something going for it in the way of good eating, with three exquisite restaurants (Julie's, Spencer's and 36 on the Quay) as well as a multitude of pubs concentrated in a small and otherwise unassuming village.

At 36 on the Quay, a warm welcome will be extended to you by a charming husband-and-wife team. Ramon Farthing's cooking is simply flawless and can best be described as innovative English/Continental cuisine. There is a six course gourmet surprise menu created to your taste (£36.50) or a three course à la carte menu, as well as an equally mouthwatering lunch menu. To complement the excellent cooking and friendly and efficient service, there is a well selected wine list with a strong emphasis on European and, particularly, classic French vintages that will certainly have something even for the refined connoisseur. Even the choice of brandies is a joy not only for francophile hedonists. It features Eau de Vie and Marc de Champagne alongside some other very good cognacs, armagnacs and calvados - served, by the way, in generous continental measures. The only drawback for yachtsmen is that this is not the place for a run ashore in dripping oilies or salty foul-weather gear; but if there is an occasion to celebrate, the chance of a romantic dinner or just the urge for a treat, this is where to set one's course.

Julie's Restaurant

30 South Street, EMSWORTH (01243) 377914

Opening Hours:

Tue-Sat	Lunch and dinner
Takeaway:	Only the bread rolls
Children:	Yes, but no children's menu
Dogs:	Can be left in the cobbled courtyard
Payment:	Cash, Visa, Mastercard or Amex

South Street is the hub of Old Emsworth and this tiny restaurant, a stone's throw from the quay, is neat, friendly and well-presented. Its name originates from a West End actress, Julie Dawncole.

The 300 year old building with cobbled courtyard was a fisherman's cottage and, it is claimed, houses a benign ghost called Fred. The food is generally Mediterranean in style with an accent on fresh local fish. The home-made bread rolls can be ordered for taking away. There is a private room which can be booked for parties.

The Old House At Home

Cottage Lane, CHIDHAM (01243) 572477

Opening Hours:

Mon-Sat	11 - 3pm, 6 - 11pm
Sundays	12 - 3pm, 7 - 10.30pm
Takeaway:	No
Children:	Yes. There is a back room for children
Dogs:	Yes
Payment:	Cash or cheque

Those who are prepared to take a walk to escape the crowd are often rewarded, and such indemnity can be found at the Old House at Home in the hamlet of Chidham. Means of access by boat are not obvious: there is a hard of sorts opposite Bosham quay, dinghies can get up Chidham creek almost to the road on a good tide, and those anchoring off Cobnor Point can probably find several places to negotiate a landing, and can then take either the public footpaths or the road to the village. Attractive footpaths run all the way round the Chidham peninsula shore, and others run inland through pleasant flat farmland at right angles to the water. If uncertain of position the twin belfried Chidham church may help, being not far from the Old House at Home. This pub building is about 300 years old, and though much renovated inside retains much of its original character. The whole roof blew off in the October '87 hurricane, leading to the discovery of a smuggler's hiding place with a cunning means of access via the chimney of the open fireplace, where a log fire is still much in use. There is a daily special on the menu, which has plenty of fish choices listed too. The food enjoys an increasingly good reputation.

Anchor Bleu

High Street, BOSHAM (01243) 573956

Opening Hours:

Mon-Sat	11 - 11pm (Bookings not taken for meals)
Sundays	Closed - except in July, August and Bank Holiday weekends when it is open 12 - 10.30pm
Takeaway:	No
Children:	No problem
Dogs:	Small dogs which fit under the tables are all right, larger dogs can be moored to the lamp post outside
Payment:	Cash, and cheque

Bosham is interesting, pretty and full of visitors in summer. The creek dries out and may have been the actual place where King Canute demonstrated that he could not hold back the tide. His daughter is allegedly buried in the churchyard.

The Anchor Bleu is a charming old waterside tavern located at Oyster Quay. It now has a new patio overlooking the harbour, plus more space at the back. The building's foundations were built by French prisoners of war which may account for the French influence in the pub's name. As one would expect in a building of its age, the pub's interior is attractively unsymmetrical. It is particularly popular with those who have come to watch the various water-based activities in the harbour and is therefore a tourist rather than a yachties' pub.

Those coming to Bosham by water may do best to berth for a small fee at the nearby quay where there is 2.5m on a neap tide for 1½ hours either side of high water. The excellent Michael McGrail is the quaymaster (01243) 573336, who says that although the quay does get full as it is used as a scrubbing berth, it is very unusual for visitors to be turned away. One can dry out alongside, and there are services such as fresh water, power and a high pressure hose. Moreover quay users, after signing the visitors book, become temporary members of the Bosham Sailing Club located just beside the quay. At high water one can arrive at the pub by dinghy, but in a storm the Anchor Bleu can be beset by heavy seas as evidenced by photos on the wall and the sturdy metal door leading to the patio, which would not be out of place in a

The Berkeley Arms Inn

Bosham Lane, OLD BOSHAM, P018 8HG (01243) 573167

Opening Hours:
Mon-Sat 11 - 3pm, 6 - 11pm
Sunday 12 - 3pm, 7 - 10.30pm
Takeaway: No
Children: Yes
Dogs: Yes
Payment: Cash, cheque, Visa, and Access

The Berkeley owes its name to a titled gentleman of that ilk and has recently been restored to its Georgian splendour. Although the pub is a 15 minute walk from the harbour, there may be occasions when - possibly having taken advantage of the handy summer ferry service from Itchenor - a foraging expedition to the farm shop on the edge of the village is called for.

One may partake either of snacks from the blackboard or the more substantial meals offered on the menu. The present landlord is himself a sailor, and both he and the landlady may be remembered by some as one-time patrons of the Fisherman's Rest in Lymington.

The Bulls Head

99 Fishbourne Road West, FISHBOURNE, Chichester PO19 3JP (01243) 785707

Opening Hours:
Weekends All day
Weekdays 11-3pm, 5.30-11pm
No food on Sunday nights
Takeaway: No
Dogs: Yes
Payment: Cash, cheques, Visa, Access

The upper, upper reaches of Fishbourne Channel are not for most owners of large deep-draughted yachts but those who have the means and skill to venture to the extreme and most northerly limit at high water by dinghy will find a small hard to the right of the channel from which access may be gained to the Bulls's Head, via a path past the old mill pond. The short and pleasant walk is enhanced if one remembers to bring some brown bread for the ducks on the pond. The Bulls Head is a Gales pub with a good selection of guest real ales to choose from. Food is in the traditional English vein with specialities of local sausages and unpasteurised cheeses, matters which should not allow one to forget the tide. There is a live jazz band on some Sundays.

Crown & Anchor

DELL QUAY, Chichester, PO21 7EB (01243) 781712

Opening Hours:

Mon-Sat	11 - 11pm
Sundays	12 - 10.30pm
Takeaway:	No
Children:	Yes
Dogs:	Yes in public bar
Payment:	Cash, cheque, Visa and Access

The eastern arm of Chichester harbour, leading up to what in Roman times was a major port at Fishbourne, is particularly beautiful but dries to a trickle at low water.

What was once the site of a Roman lookout post is now that of the Crown and Anchor, the present building being very old with a murky history of smuggling and retribution. It certainly has a priest's hole of Elizabethan vintage and possibly a ghost. The outlook over the creek is lovely and there is a choice of bars. The snug public bar is of most interest to yachtsmen, with a log fire in an ancient fireplace, good photographs of J-Class racing yachts, local craft, local buildings and also instruments giving prevailing wind speed and direction. The pub has its own mooring, but there is over 4m on a good tide alongside the end of the quay where one can dry out on a firm bottom, while those with friends in the admirable Dell Quay Sailing Club may be able to arrange alternative accommodation for their vessel. There is also a public hard north of the quay.

It should be mentioned that, if planning to stay at Dell Quay over the tide, or if of shallow draft, one can get up to Fishbourne either by the footpath beside the creek or by sea. Although 1½ miles distant there are not only the Roman excavations to see, but other pleasing taverns to be found, such as the Bulls Head where thirst may be quenched.

The Blacksmith's Arms

Selsey Road, DONNINGTON PO20 7PR (01243) 783999

Opening Hours:
Weekdays 11 - 2.30pm, 6 - 11pm
Sundays 12 - 3pm, 7 - 10.30pm
Takeaway: No
Children : Yes
Dogs: Yes
Payment: Cash or cheque, no credit cards

Visitors and inhabitants of Chichester Marina, perhaps awaiting the tide for the lock, who might enjoy a one and a half mile walk before their repast, should visit The Blacksmith's Arms. Take the footpath running beside the Chichester Canal on the south side of the marina and proceed eastwards. Cross the main road and carry on to the next road, turn to starboard down this road onto a course of about 235° and after a quarter of a mile the pub will be found on the right. One should not need a hand-held GPS for this endeavour but those navigators who like to leave nothing to chance can note that the pub lies at 50°48.40N and 0°47.50W.

The Blacksmith's Arms, dating from 1730, used to serve canal traffic until the canal was closed in 1906. Before then one could get from Chichester to London by barge. At the front of the pub there is a 300 year old box tree, thought to be the oldest in England, and at the rear there is a garden hedged with damson trees, a legacy from the time when the garden was part of an orchard. In the middle of the pub will be found traditional home-cooked food in the restaurant, several well-kept real ales, table service to the garden and a very good 'little peoples' menu for children.

If the hand-held GPS is thought to be necessary on the way home, the co-ordinates of the nearest end of the marina are 50°48.12N and 0°47.90W.

The Spinnaker

Chichester Marina, BIRDHAM, Sussex PO20 7EJ (01243) 5110323

Opening Hours:
8.30 - 11pm
Takeaway: Just give your ship's complement and name your destination
Children: There is a children's play area
Dogs: No
Payment: Cash, cheque, Visa, Access, Amex

The Spinnaker is a modern, glass-fronted building set in pleasant surroundings overlooking Chichester Marina, and is run by a couple who have done 60,000 miles under sail in their 50 foot ketch, this including four transatlantic crossings.

As experienced sailors they aim to cater for the usual requirements for both visiting and indigenous sailors all year round They will serve breakfast until noon, lunch, tea and dinner, either in the conservatory bar/restaurant or the patio garden. They will provide groceries, beer, wines and spirits, bagged ice, magazines and daily newspapers, and indeed victual a whole boat bound for distant waters. Moreover they have a launderette which can be put to good use whilst enjoying the facilities. Landlubbers and party bookings are welcome.

The Ship

High Street, ITCHENOR (01243) 512284
Harbourmaster's office: (01243) 512301 or Channel 14

Opening Hours:
Variable with the season, best to phone if coming from afar
Takeaway: No
Children: Yes
Dogs: Yes
Payment: Cash or cheque

Itchenor was once quite a sea port and shipbuilding centre, moreover Charles II found it an agreeable site for both his yacht and lady friend. Nowadays Itchenor is entirely given over to yachts and leisure pursuits, and with an attractive village and ancient church, is well worth a visit. Mooring and temporary alongside arrangements should be made with the harbour master's office when visiting Itchenor, his office being on the hard.

The well known, large but welcoming Ship Inn will be found after a short walk inland which provides the focus and convivial surroundings for both local and passing yachtsmen. Landlady Pam Mesham does the home prepared and cooked food, duly advertised upon two blackboards, and there are plenty of tables both outside and inside. There are three double bedrooms available. One cannot fail to notice the decorative array of chamber pots which numbered 44 at the last count.

It is worth mentioning that a summer ferry service runs between Itchenor and Bosham, which will collect from moorings and can be contacted through the harbour master's office.

Fox's Restaurant

11 High Street, BEMBRIDGE, Isle of Wight PO35 5SD (01983) 872626

Opening Hours:

Lunch	Weekday 12 - 1.45 pm
	Sunday 1.15pm
Dinner	7.15 - 9pm last orders
	Closed Mondays
Takeaway:	No
Children:	Yes
Dogs:	No
Payment:	Cash, Visa, Access, and Amex
Taxi:	(01983) 874132 / 811666

The small and intimate Fox's Restaurant specialises in locally caught fish; and has rightly won a reputation within Bembridge for good value and a pleasant atmosphere, though many clients come from far afield. Tony Monk does all the cooking which he describes as a composite of English, French and Italian. He was once a Falmouth boat-builder and owner of a Yeti class International 14 called *Snowmist* but now sails a Solo. At one time Ann and Tony Monk ran the New Inn at Shalfleet, this being Ann's home country, but gave it up to start their own thing in Bembridge. A measure of their success is the need to book for weekend dinners and Sunday lunch-times literally a week ahead in summer. Fox's, which owes its name to the one time licensed premises on the same site called the Fox's Head, will be found opposite Lloyd's bank, after a short walk up King's Road from the embankment to the square formed by the High Street, Sherbourne Street and Church Road. Lovers of antique ordnance will enjoy Fox's collection, and those who feel that exercise does them more harm than good should take a taxi up the hill.

The Crab & Lobster Inn

The Forelands, BEMBRIDGE, Isle of Wight PO35 5TR (01983) 872244

Opening Hours:

Jul-Sep	All day Fri, Sat & Sun
Other times	11 - 3pm, 6 - 11pm
Takeaway:	No
Children:	Yes, except for main bar area. No special facilities
Dogs:	No special facilities
Payment:	Cash, cheque, Visa, Access & Switch
Taxi:	Barry (01983) 874132; Ralph (01983) 811666

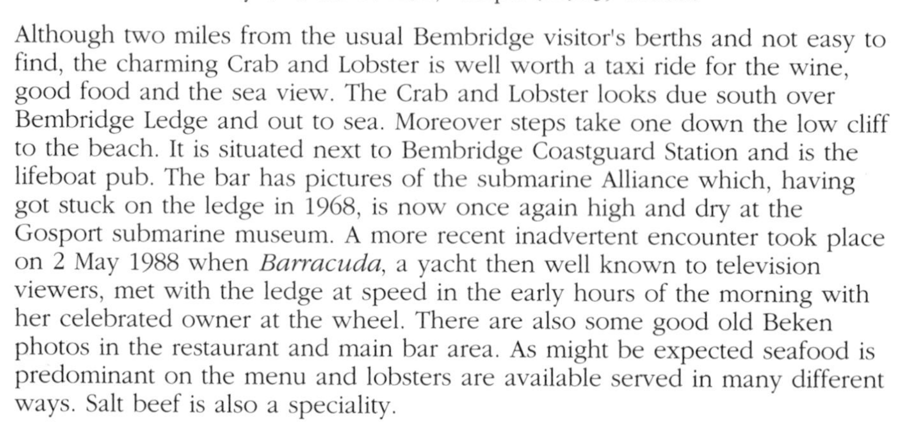

Although two miles from the usual Bembridge visitor's berths and not easy to find, the charming Crab and Lobster is well worth a taxi ride for the wine, good food and the sea view. The Crab and Lobster looks due south over Bembridge Ledge and out to sea. Moreover steps take one down the low cliff to the beach. It is situated next to Bembridge Coastguard Station and is the lifeboat pub. The bar has pictures of the submarine Alliance which, having got stuck on the ledge in 1968, is now once again high and dry at the Gosport submarine museum. A more recent inadvertent encounter took place on 2 May 1988 when *Barracuda*, a yacht then well known to television viewers, met with the ledge at speed in the early hours of the morning with her celebrated owner at the wheel. There are also some good old Beken photos in the restaurant and main bar area. As might be expected seafood is predominant on the menu and lobsters are available served in many different ways. Salt beef is also a speciality.

The Pilot Boat Inn

Station Road, BEMBRIDGE, Isle of Wight (01983) 872077

Takeaway:	See below
Children:	Yes
Dogs:	Yes
Payment:	Cash, cheques

The Pilot Boat Inn is only a few steps from the harbour and is instantly recognisable owing to its strikingly original maritime outside appearance and the carved figurehead above the door. It is a delightfully unpretentious, some might say slightly shabby pub, frequented by locals and yachtsmen alike and a refreshing change from the many streamlined brewer's pubs. In keeping with the style, the food is simple but good: salads, burgers, baguettes, steaks, fish, sandwiches are all available. There are also children's dishes. The easygoing attitude of this friendly place may be illustrated by the laconic answer to the question as to whether takeaway food was available: 'Sure - if anyone wants to take it away with them, no problem!'

The Square Rigger

Sherbourne Street, BEMBRIDGE, Isle of Wight (01983) 872734

Restaurant Opening Hours:

Summer	10am - 10pm
Other times	Lunchtime only
Takeaway:	Yes
Children:	Yes
Dogs:	No
Payment:	Cash, cheque, Access and Visa

Visitors to Bembridge Harbour may be tempted to visit the village of Bembridge itself, which involves an interesting walk along Embankment Road and up King's Road. In the centre of the village will be found the Square Rigger, a friendly family restaurant. No-nonsense, traditional English food is cooked here, with daily specials and an emphasis on fresh fish providing a good choice. Many yachtsmen may find the remarkable collection of yachting photographs from the 1880's, which adorn the walls of the dining room, with more to be found in a dedicated upstairs exhibition room, of particular interest. These are all prints made from the original glass plates which were found quite by chance, and most of these images of a bygone era are truly fascinating.

The Vine Inn

Upper Green Road, ST HELENS, Isle of Wight PO33 1UJ (01983) 872337

Opening Hours:

Weekdays	11 - 11pm
Sundays	12 - 10.30pm
Takeaway:	Chicken curry, given notice
Children:	Yes
Dogs:	Yes
Payment:	Cash, cheque

If walking up the hill to St Helens from Bembridge one may notice the Vine Inn across the green, especially if a live band is performing, as it does on Thursday nights. This pub attracts its clientele widely from the Island with each night tending to have its special crowd. The younger element tend to congregate at the back where there is a pool table, juke box, one armed bandits, Sky TV etc. and the more mature at the more peaceful front. There is now a café attached to the pub, approachable down a side alley or through the pub building.

After climbing the hill one may feel that a drink is both welcome and deserved, besides giving an opportunity to enjoy a bit of local colour.

The Old Fort

Esplanade, SEAVIEW (01983) 612363

Opening Hours:

Mon-Sat	11 - 11pm
Sundays	12 - 10.30pm
Takeaway:	No
Children:	Restaurant area only
Dogs:	Yes on a lead
Payment:	Cash, cheque, Access or Visa

Seaview is often sheltered and sunny when other places are not so nice, but beware an easterly swell. When anchoring, or getting a mooring through the Seaview Yacht Club's boatman who will take one ashore as well, the landing points are found just opposite The Old Fort. This is built on the site of a fort presumably built to guard the eastern Solent. From here one can look over to Hampshire, watch the busy shipping besides one's own craft at rest. The premises were refurbished in 1996 and the proprietor is a Seaview local who is involved with powerboating, windsurfing etc. There is live music at weekends.

Seaview Hotel & Restaurant

High Street, SEAVIEW PO34 5EX (01983) 612711

Restaurant Opening Hours:

12.45 - 1.30pm, 7.30 - 9.15pm
Closed Sunday night except bank holidays

Children:	Yes and babies, but no children under five in the restaurants in the evening
Dogs:	Well behaved quiet dogs welcome but not in the restaurants
Payment:	Cash, cheque, Amex, Switch, Diners, Access and Visa

There is a particularly attractive atmosphere about the east-facing seaside village of Seaview, and landing is no problem thanks to the kind services of the Seaview Yacht Club ferry service, which can be arranged through the hotel or on (01983) 613268. There are several bars of which the Pump Room, with an open fire in winter, is generally used by locals and yachtsmen, and a new second restaurant. The cocktail bar at the front, which opens out onto a patio overlooking the sea, has a fine collection of pictures of warships and liners, the warships being of special interest to the author who, with his father, can claim to have served upon several of them. The imaginative bar food is quite different from normal, for example local crab with cheese and spices cooked under a grill, scallops sautéed with fresh tarragon, and fresh whole Bembridge lobsters; but the most attractive feature of all is the pretty little restaurant and remarkably high quality food which has understandably won numerous accolades.

The Ryde Castle

The Esplanade, RYDE, Isle of Wight (01983) 563755

Opening Hours:
All day
Takeaway: No
Children: Yes
Dogs: No
Payment: Cash, cheque and all credit cards except Switch

The new Ryde Harbour has brought Ryde more into the boating scene, and the modest dues are consistent with the fact that it dries right out at low water. As with many venues mentioned in this book, one needs to be very careful regarding the tide if one's boat is not designed to dry out comfortably. That said Ryde, as a watering hole, will be new to most and may be a place of interest for that reason.

Access to the harbour is approximately between two hours either side of high water by way of the well-marked channel. Two amber depth indicator lights are directed down this channel, and when the lower one shows there is at least one metre within the harbour, and when both upper and lower amber lights are showing there is at least one and a half metres within the harbour. Deep keel yachts can dry out alongside the quay and those able to take the ground without falling over, or those only staying over high water, can use the pontoon nearest the quay which is intended for visitors. There are berths for seventy visiting craft and the Harbourmaster may be reached on Channel 80, call-sign 'Ryde Harbour'. Beware of hovercraft and ferries in the approach to the channel.

For sustenance one can do a lot worse than by visiting The Ryde Castle. This is the grand and rather splendid hotel to the right of the marina, past the bowling green nestling, perhaps slightly uncomfortably, with the paraphernalia of a seaside resort. There are hot and cold snacks at the bar, with 25 fillings to choose from if one orders sandwiches. The restaurant is good for more substantial meals at reasonable cost.

Platter's Café

106A Monkton Street, RYDE, Isle of Wight   No Telephone

Opening Hours:

Fri, Sat	9 - 2.30pm, 6 - 9pm
Sunday	10 - 2.30pm
Takeaway:	Yes
Children:	Yes
Dogs:	No
Payment:	Cash, cheques

The Platter's Café is a good little traditional café running an all day breakfast, but with evening food available too. It is well run and attracts those marina users who know Ryde well. One is encouraged to bring one's own wine for evening meals.

From the main entrance of the marina, go through the gardens, cross The Esplanade thence 100m down Monkton Street. Dover Street is one street to the west and Cornwallis Street one too far to the east. There is a sign up at the marina.

Fishbourne Inn

Fishbourne Lane, WOOTTON   (01983) 882823
Royal Victoria Yacht Club   (01983) 882325

Opening Hours:

Mon-Sat	11 - 3pm, 6 - 11pm
Sundays	12 - 3pm, 7 - 10.30pm
Takeaway:	No
Children:	Yes
Dogs:	Dogs should be on a lead, and are not allowed into the restaurant
Payment:	Cash or cheque

The Fishbourne Inn is to be found nestling in the trees just to the east of the car ferry terminal. Given the right conditions, it is possible to anchor off the beach, but landing may present complications so it may be preferable to get advice on a mooring from the Royal Victoria Yacht Club, where visiting yachtsmen are made welcome. One will, of course, not be at all popular anchoring in the fairway. The food at the Fishbourne, being grills and locally caught seafood in summer, has a very good reputation on the Island, more than justifying the short walk round the ferry terminal. In fine weather one can eat outside and enjoy the well kept garden.

The Sloop Inn

WOOTTON BRIDGE (01983) 882544

Restaurant Opening Hours:
Mon-Sat 11.30am - 10pm
Sundays 12 noon - 10pm
Takeaway: No
Children: Yes - good facilities for children and families
Dogs: No
Payment: Cash, cheque, Access and Visa

The tranquil and mainly wooded Wootton Creek is the home of many interesting old vessels, and though the voyage up Wootton Creek may look a little daunting on the chart, small craft moorings and navigational buoys give assistance to pilotage. Vessels unable to take the mud should be very cautious, but shallow draught craft will have little trouble, as the channel has 4 metres of water at high tide. The last hour of the flood tide is recommended for a first visit, and one can get right up to the bridge at Wootton where two public landing places will be found beside the Sloop Inn. Dinghies and small craft will also be able to tie up to the rings on the pub wall, with a depth of over one metre at high water.

The Sloop is a large pub, one of the over 300 in the Brewers Fayre chain, which especially caters for families with young children - there is even a toddler's play area, an outside children's play area with a bouncy castle (summer only) and a full children's menu. The large but rather standard menu is enriched by a selection of house specials, and on fine summer days the food will best be enjoyed in the garden overlooking the creek.

God's Providence House

St. Thomas' Square, NEWPORT (01983) 522085

Opening Hours:
Mon-Sat 9 - 5pm
Closed on Sundays
Takeaway: Yes
Children: Yes
Dogs: No
Payment: Cash, cheque, credit cards

This is a well established, old fashioned family restaurant in the centre of Newport and something of a local institution, catering for lunches and afternoon teas, with snacks and light meals served all day. The luncheons are in the traditional English style, but reasonably priced, the snacks include salads, sandwiches, jackets, quiches and similar bites. The wine list is somewhat limited, but at least this establishment is not totally dry. The afternoon teas are popular for the variety of homemade cakes and scones.

Moulin Rouge

St. Thomas' Square, NEWPORT, Isle of Wight (01983) 530001

Opening Hours:
8am - 11pm
(Meals 11 - 3pm, 6 - 9.30pm)
Closed on Sundays
Takeaway: No
Children: Yes, until 6 or 7pm
Dogs: Yes, if well behaved
Payment: Cash, cheque, credit cards

This newly opened, French style Café and Bar is a welcome addition to the gastronomic scene of Newport: 'France on the Isle of Wight', maybe an alternative for frustrated sailors whose channel crossing has been prevented by bad weather or lack of time. In any case, this refreshing café offers a good range of aperitifs, wines, coffees, snacks and light meals à la Française. Salads (including the French classic chevre chaud), hors d'oeuvres, steak frites, quiches, coq-au-vin and entrecotes in sauce poivre. This is enough to make any francophile feel comfortably at home. Located in the centre of Newport, it is only a few minutes walk from the river.

The Classic Boat Café

Seaclose Wharf, Town Quay, NEWPORT, Isle of Wight (01983) 533493

Opening Hours:
10.30 - 4.30pm
Days closed: Christmas night
Takeaway: Yes
Children: Yes
Dogs: Only if quiet and well behaved
Payment: Cash

The Classic Boat Museum has been established on The Quay in Newport thanks to the private initiative of two sailors with the enthusiasm for restoring classic craft. The small museum has a fine and changing collection of steamboats, runabouts and sailing dinghies, also featuring engines, photographs and general nautical memorabilia. The majority of boats on display are in working order and frequently used, which is the best way of keeping them in top condition. The visiting yachtsman may also be interested in the loft of traditional sailmakers Ratsey & Lapthorn which is directly opposite on the same quay. The friendly café is situated in the entrance area of the Classic Boat Museum and offers a range of sandwiches and hot food including daily specials at very reasonable prices - a main meal with dessert costs around £3.50 - cream teas and children's dishes. There is also plenty of literature about the boats to help pass the time in the café. As the premises is not licensed, customers may import their own supplies which may be obtained at the Riverside Centre on The Quay.

Tony's

21-22 High Street, NEWPORT, Isle of Wight (01983) 527054

Opening Hours:
Restaurant 9am - 9pm
Takeaway 11.30pm
Takeaway: Yes. The takeaway is at 22 High street and provides a speedy service
Children: Children welcome
Dogs: No
Payment: Cash or cheque

There are three Tony's licensed restaurants on the Island, but the one most likely to be useful to yachtsman is in Newport next door to Coleman's Bookshop. They are clearly well run and represent very good value in terms of price, quality and quantity. For example at the time of writing one can have a three course set meal including steak for £7.75. Over a hundred items of food are available and there is a special Sunday menu.

INDEX